A NATION DIVIDED

A NATION DIVIDED

Problems and Issues of the Civil War and Reconstruction

EDITED BY

George M. Fredrickson

Northwestern University
Evanston, Illinois

BURGESS PUBLISHING COMPANY • MINNEAPOLIS, MINNESOTA

To the Memory of
Alexander K. Fraser

Copyright © 1975 by Burgess Publishing Company
Printed in the United States of America
Library of Congress Catalog Card Number 74-27235
ISBN 0-8087-0624-1

2   3   4   5   6   7   8   9   10

Contents

GEORGE M. FREDRICKSON

Introduction

THE CIVIL WAR is the most written-about subject in American history. But of the thousands of books and articles on the conflict and its aftermath, only a very small percentage go beyond a description of particular events or personalities and try to give a coherent sense of what the war was all about. In this volume six historians confront some of the larger questions that have to be resolved before a real understanding of the Civil War and Reconstruction can be achieved. Although a good deal of factual information is imparted, the stress is on interpretation of major issues and not on a systematic, textbook-type coverage of the period. It is hoped that the essays will stimulate and inform the student while at the same time presenting fresh ideas that will be of interest to other historians and to that segment of the general reading public that seeks fuller comprehension of a critical episode in our national experience.

The focus is on the public drama of sectional conflict or, as the title suggests, on the theme of "a nation divided." Crucial related subjects—such as the institution of slavery, the abolitionist movement, race relations, and the general social and economic conditions of the time—are not discussed extensively but are treated mainly as background to the behavior of politicians and policy makers. But this does not mean that the contributors are last-ditch adherents to the view that history is simply "past politics." The

1

public decisions that led to the Civil War, determined its outcome and consequences, and set the pattern for national reunification are considered central in the sense that these are what historians are most obligated to explain. As the reader will quickly see, the explanations offered tend to go beyond politics in the narrow sense and involve a consideration of ideological, cultural, and socioeconomic conditions. But for a comprehensive and detailed understanding of these conditions, the reader must turn to specialized studies in the social, economic, and intellectual history of the period.

The essays are arranged in a roughly chronological fashion, although there is some overlap. The first two are concerned mainly with the background and origins of the war, the third pursues the relationship of Lincoln and the Negro through both the prewar and war years, the fourth focuses on the war itself, and the last two deal with Reconstruction. As has been suggested, no attempt has been made to describe and analyze all the significant events of the period. Each essayist has been free to develop a particular theme and has introduced only such factual material as was relevant to his interpretation of a particular issue. Nevertheless, a major portion of the essential history of what occurred during these years does emerge. Although not intended to be a general introduction to the history of the Civil War and Reconstruction, this volume can serve that purpose if the reader is also willing to consult a textbook or narrative account to fill in gaps and illuminate references.

Besides telling part of a larger story, each essay can be seen as a distinct variation of the theme of "a nation divided." William W. Freehling sees the division between North and South as an example of what happens in a democratic society when the will of a majority clashes directly with a minority's determination to protect its special interests at any cost, even if it destroys national unity in the process. Eric Foner examines the political effects of the ideological cleavage between the defenders of southern slavery and the proponents of northern free labor and concludes that the inability of the American party system to deal with this kind of ideological polarization set the stage for a violent confrontation. Taking the conflict over slavery as a point of departure, Don E. Fehrenbacher concerns himself with how the sectional division related to another way in which the nation was (and is) divided—between black and white. In a discussion of Lincoln's racial attitudes and policies, he sheds light on the role of the race issue in the politics of the period and on the kind of leadership Lincoln provided. My essay starts from the point where political separation has occurred and examines the wartime policies of North and South in an effort to explain why the struggle turned out the way it did. William R. Brock describes and analyzes the attempts made during Reconstruction to restore the prewar two-party system as a basis of national integration and provides an explanation of why these efforts failed. Focusing on the Reconstruction process in the South, Otto H. Olsen argues that enduring cultural differences between the sections doomed to failure the Republican effort to remake the South in accordance with northern ideals and values.

If the entire volume has a message it would have to be that the divisions sundering the nation in the "middle period" of its history were more profound and durable than many historians have been willing to acknowledge. The differences between the Old North and Old South were not of a sort that could be resolved by the American political system as it normally operates. When the issue was carried to the battlefield, the divergent nature of the two societies had an important effect on the war's outcome, and the decisive victory of the North signified the death of slavery and national reunification under northern leadership. But even war and the extraordinary measures of Reconstruction could not obliterate sectional and racial distinctions. The preservation of the Union, in other words, did not bring an end to national division. But it did mean that the continuing conflicts resulting from region and race would have to be resolved in some other way than by the clash of armies.

WILLIAM W. FREEHLING

Nullification,
Minority Blackmail,
and the Crisis of Majority Rule

THEY DID NOT LOOK LIKE an oppressed minority.

The fastidiously dressed squires, fresh from bouts at the feasting table, swaggered up to embattled Charleston Bay. Retinues of black slaves trailed respectfully at a distance. Peering across the water, white knights scoffed at plebeians in federal forts. It seemed hardly worth a gentleman's time to blast the rabble out.

To hear John C. Calhoun tell it, these South Carolina slaveholders were themselves enslaved. The scruffy soldiers training federal guns on Charleston were agents of majority despotism. The polished patricians pushing to give President Jackson his come-uppance were verging on extinction. Jackson's notion that he was but preserving the majority's right to ·make law was nonsense. Unless oppressed minorities could nullify illegitimate majoritarian law, democracy would become but "might makes right." In that case, the rich and mighty would fall. America could become the land of the scummy herd.

The South Carolina nullifiers' notion that the rich need protection from the poor was nothing new under the American sun. It had informed much Federalist rhetoric and some Jeffersonian. It

was endemic to the conservative outcry of ultra-Whigs like Phillip
Hone no less than to the extremist measures of John C. Calhoun.
Men of property will ever tremble that the democratic beast could
get out of hand.

But what thrust nullifiers into shivering isolation was the way
they defined minority interest. Their exalted minority was not an
embattled upper class. It was not even the planter segment of the
American upper class. It was a fragment of a fragment of a
fragment. Theirs was the notion that tiny and isolated extremes
should give law to massive majorities. They lost. They won in the
losing. Their victory commenced a trail of victories which threw
the very meaning of majority rule in doubt.

ONE

The grand crisis in ideology started as a provincial battle over
taxes. In 1828 and again in 1832, national congressional majorities
passed high protective tariffs. South Carolina planters, aware that
discouraging imports would discourage cotton and rice exports,
believed that southern exporters would slide towards bankruptcy.
High tariffs, they urged, violated the Constitution. Moreover, if a
northern high tariff majority could trample on the Constitution,
southern minorities had no constitutional protection against antislavery laws.

South Carolina's peculiar social structure led to an early and
acute sensitivity to such problems. The more ocean-bound, lower
half of the state was a dense, malaria-infested swamp kept from
relapsing into jungle by a veritable army of slaves. A ten-to-one
ratio of blacks to whites typified most low-country areas. Improved land costs of $100 per acre were common. Allow emanci-
pation, everyone believed, and the white slaveholder's most fabu-
lous kingdom would become a genuine African jungle.

The upper half of the state, in contrast, was the Cotton South's
most degenerating empire. Up-country Carolina, as the first Deep
South recipient of the Eli Whitney cotton-gin bonanza, was also
the first to gut its soil. Whereas every other Deep South state was
clearing land, buying slaves, and flexing muscles like an audacious
adolescent, up-country Carolinians were abandoning plantations,
hemorrhaging away population, and wailing about ebbing vitality.

The two halves of South Carolina, taken together, were the
oldest of Deep South states, the most unified, the most proud, the
most aristocratic, the most declining, the most frightened, and the

most convulsively committed. Such characteristics goaded Carolinians to spy monopolists and abolitionists where other southerners saw but the thin air. Some lethal weapon, Carolina nabobs believed, had to be found to rouse the South and rout the North.

The best weapon available was John C. Calhoun's doctrine of nullification. Vice President Calhoun, in a secret report to the South Carolina legislature in 1828, had argued that no arm of the federal government had final power to interpret the Constitution. Otherwise, minorities would be powerless. Majorities elected the Congress and the President; and a majoritarian President could conspire with a majoritarian Congress to place majoritarian judges on the Supreme Court. The final judge of constitutional issues, Calhoun affirmed, must be the state conventions which had originally adopted the Constitution. Every significant minority could control at least one state. If any one state could declare unconstitutional laws null and void, King Law would replace King Numbers. Majorities would rule without trampling on minorities.

In November of 1832, a South Carolina convention gave Calhoun's theories practical expression. The convention declared the federal tariff laws of 1828 and 1932 null and void in South Carolina. Attempts to collect duties by force would be resisted by force. The minority had spoken. The majority must halt.

President Andrew Jackson, recently swept into office for a second term by a heady majority, had no intention of halting. He ordered reinforcements into Charleston Harbor. He secured a Force Bill from Congress. The majority, he said, must rule. The Union, he proclaimed, must be preserved.

Some South Carolina hotheads were in fact aching to bust up the Union. Calhoun was not of their number. The Vice President, now resigning to become Senator from South Carolina, considered his brainchild the only way to preserve the Union. If fire-eaters like his brethren had no protection against majoritarian slavery and tariff outrages, the Union would eventually be smashed. Fanatical minorities would unceremoniously walk out of uncontrolled democracies. At issue was more than the legitimacy of majorities. At stake was the very survival of working democracy.

TWO

While the two armies in Charleston Harbor oiled their guns, statesmen in Washington tried to maintain a ceasefire. In both cities, crisis conditions mocked Calhoun's theories. The Carolina planter class emerged as a majoritarian despot at home and an extremely powerful minority of a minority abroad.

The very rhetoric of slaveholders calling themselves enslaved called attention to Calhoun's incongruous position as minority spokeman. To slaveholders, no incongruity existed. Only blacks were slaves. Only whites were citizens. Only citizens had rights.

The broader issue, however, could not be wiped out by narrow racism. Nullification was intentionally a way to spike reform legislation, and an entrenched upper class could use the dogma to keep fellow citizens eating the dirt. Nullification made sense if only government oppressed minorities. If government action alone could end minority oppression, nullification perpetuated majority despotism. Blacks being sold at auction within sight of a planter's army in the breech against antislavery threw Carolina's theories forever into shambles.

The anti-nullification minority in South Carolina no less mocked nullification as minority salvation. Non-slaveholding yeomen in up-country mountains and non-slaveholding merchants in Charleston eagerly volunteered for Jackson's army. They had no other protection against being jailed as traitors for minority protests against Calhoun's majoritarian dictatorship at home. They had every intention of showing Mr. Calhoun that minorities had rights even within a nullifier's kingdom.

While protests in South Carolina undermined Calhoun's position as minority spokesman, protests from other southern states exploded his position as representative of a planter minority. Most southern planters thought nullification extreme. They had not yet lost hope that the majority would lower the tariff. They were not yet sure slavery was in danger. They disliked the notion that majority will becomes law only when every minority of a minority agrees. Calhoun had called nullification viable because every interest controlled one state. In fact, the plantation minority controlled many states and hoped nullification would be repudiated.

Calhoun's theories thus seemed to unravel wherever messy reality intruded. The supposedly enslaved minority was itself one of the world's greatest slaveholders. The allegedly helpless national minority was a tyrannical state majority. The supposed representative of planter interest was wildly unrepresentative. What with opposition in Carolina and outrage elsewhere, the arch nullifier seemed destined for a noose as he headed into Jackson's Washington. Instead, he all but dictated terms of a settlement. He thus gave the coup de grace to his own notion of powerless minorities.

Calhoun's victory was obscured, not least to Calhoun himself, by Jackson's demolition of nullification. Congress, in the Force Bill, gave the President all necessary power to make South Carolina obey the law. The Force Bill was a perpetual national monument warning that state veto would never be tolerated.

But Congress also lowered the tariff Carolina had called intolerable. The majority gave in and passed the Compromise Tariff of 1833 partly because most Americans wanted lower tariffs anyway. The high tariff laws of earlier Congress were overdue for overhauling. In a nation of exporting farmers, free trade easily became sacred text.

But the majority acted at this particular time because nullifiers had successfully deployed an extremist's classic strategy. The extremist's curse is always that most men on his side are moderates. His hope is to create a confrontation situation where moderates are forced off the fence. The moderate's classic response is to defuse confrontation by arranging a compromise. While extremists fume if compromise succeeds, history has at least been wrenched a bit in their direction. If compromise fails, extremists are in the saddle. Moderates on their side can only choose which army to join.

In nullification times and long thereafter, the institution best able to keep armies on the sidelines was Jackson's National Democratic party. While the Democratic party was the nation's majority party, the majorities were disproportionately large in the Deep South. Non-Carolina planters, if embarrassed by their lunatic fringe, had no desire to annihilate fellow slaveholders. Carolina nullifiers were, after all, but expressing an embarrassing extreme of southern anti-tariff and anti-abolition tendencies. In the nullification winter, southern Democrats urged compromise. Northern Democrats were anxious to keep party and union together. A compromise tariff passed with Andrew Jackson's blessings. An extremist group threatening to bring off war had demonstrated the awesome power of blackmailer.

In one sense, the successful blackmail vindicated Calhoun's exploded theory. He had urged that democracy would collapse if potentially secessionist extremes were left dangerously disgruntled. President Jackson and the American majority had indirectly accepted that logic. Revolutionary extremes must be appeased if the democratic consensus is to endure. The majority's own desire for tariff reform had made the appeasement of 1833 easy. But how would the system work when the blackmailer demanded that majority give noxious appeasement? And how could democracy survive if the blackmailer was not appeased?

THREE

The ensuing thirty years of American history would provide answers to those questions. The answers were enough to make democrats anywhere tremble. Americans like to think of themselves as inhabitants of a City on the Hill, providentially destined to show a sinning world how to achieve salvation through democracy. Alas, in 1861, they demonstrated that democracy sometimes works only if God is on the side of the strongest battalions. The explosion of the American government came about not because of blundering statesmen. Rather, the democratic system proved unable to withstand strains which had placed Jackson and Calhoun at each other's throats.

In the years after nullification, the Carolina position that the world was closing in on slavery became slowly more plausible to others in the Cotton South. The South was ever more clearly in a permanent minority. Abolition was ever more surely sweeping bondage from Latin America. Abolitionists were ever more stridently demanding action from the North. Yankees, although with massive misgivings, showed signs of someday listening. Some southern areas, particularly in the more northern South, showed signs of someday surrendering. If Deep South slaveholders were to avoid becoming the last of a vanishing breed, proslavery perpetualists saw need to blast the tendencies of history aside.

In pre-Civil War years, as in 1832, South Carolina remained self-appointed king of the blasters. Calhoun's state continued to suffer from a terminal case of southern claustrophobia. In the Carolina view of the world, abolition meant anarchy. Free blacks spelled unspeakable bloodbath. Giving in to an age of antislavery meant surrendering the right to drink, eat, and breathe. Such hidebound reactionaries are beyond soothing. Their antennas register the softest hint of danger, and American antislavery hints were not the softest. No matter how often the northern majority indicated willingness to let well enough alone, southern extremists could not forget what the northern minority wanted—and where an age of romantic democracy was drifting.

Again and again, plantation ultras sought to nullify their age. They did not call it nullification. Jackson's Force Bill had made state veto disreputable. But nullification as a power play had little to do with state veto. The iron behind Calhoun's velvet was the threat of secession, and that threat, emanating especially from South Carolina, became a great staple of American antebellum politics.

In prewar years, as in the nullification confrontation, southern ultras gained power by taking normal southern fears to an extreme. Everywhere in southern plantation black belts, men worried about "holier-than-thou" northerners and about secretly disloyal southerners. Throughout the slaveholding South, bondage was considered the bulwark keeping black men this side of barbarism. Accordingly, whenever southern extremists sought to bring off confrontation, southern moderates used the occasion to demand concessions. Northern Democrats continued to consider appeasing the demand patriotism to party and country. The plantation South thus had the leverage of the nation's majority party. The ultimatums of a few helped turn democracy into minority rule.

The first post-nullification ultimatum came three years after nullification had supposedly been nullified. In 1835, southerners demanded that Congress gag discussion of slavery. If a Gag Rule was not passed, warned a minority of the southern minority, the South would smash the Union. Southern Democrats demanded concessions. Northern Democrats obliged. A Gag Rule was passed.

In 1850, southerners demanded that Congress force northerners to return alleged fugitive slaves without a prior jury trial. Even if a Fugitive Slave Law was passed, warned a minority of the southern minority, South Carolina and a couple of other states would try to smash the Union. Northern Democrats and more moderate southerners wished to isolate so ferocious an extreme. A Fugitive Slave Law was passed.

In 1854, southerners demanded that Congress repeal the sanctified Missouri Compromise and open the plains of Kansas to the possibility of enslavement. Again, the minority threatened. Again, southern Democrats demanded. Again, northern Democrats acquiesced.

But the northern Democrats' cave-in came with escalating outrage. Northerners, watching a system supposedly based on majority rule continually yield minority triumphs, came to believe a conspiracy was sabotaging democracy. A slave-power conspiracy, so the Yankee argument went, was demolishing the system and had to be stopped. The way to stop the conspiracy was to replace the Democratic party.

After 1854, a Republican party opposition grew like a hurricane in the North. Northern Democrats, trapped between southern demands and constituents' disgust, found their numbers drastically dwindling in Congress. They came to believe, along with their Republican opponents, that it was high time to call the black-mailers' bluff.

The bluff was first called in 1860. At the national Democratic party convention in Charleston, southern extremists demanded that the party endorse slave protection in national territories. Otherwise, said William L. Yancey and fellow spirits, they would walk out. Northern Democrats said nay. Yancey walked. Only a minority of southern delegates followed. They were enough to set in motion a stream of party combat that savaged the last major, national, pre-Civil War party.

During the ensuing national presidential canvass, many Deep South planters urged secession if Abraham Lincoln won. Lincoln won. The southern majority then wished to wait and see if Lincoln tried overt antislavery acts. The minority of the southern minori-ty, particularly in South Carolina, had waited too long. South Carolina's secession was enough to set in motion a stream of national disintegration which could only end in trial by war. The extremists at last had their delicious confrontation. Southerners in the middle could choose no more than whether to fire at Yankees or Southrons.

Lincoln, casting himself in Andrew Jackson's image, said that democracy and majority rule must be preserved. The Deep South, proving John C. Calhoun a prophet, said that a minority without protection must willy-nilly preserve itself. Both sides had shown that democracy was damned if it did or didn't. A faction with the will and power to destroy inevitably impaled the republic on one horn of the dilemma. Either the majority gave in to the black-mailer—and thus surrendered a majority's right to rule—or the majority acted like a majority—and thereby called the black-mailers' bluff. As Calhoun had known, these blackmailers were not bluffing. The republic crashed to the delight of anti-democrats around the globe.

FOUR

The delight was short-lived. Lincoln's armies succeeded. Might saved "right." The crash became a romance. Americans went on believing republicanism would save the world. They forgot that Satan sometimes commands the largest battalions. No American minority has again tried the blackmail of secession. One lesson of Appomattox has never been forgotten. As long as majorities command the strongest armies, seceding minorities are architects of their own doom.

But one does not have to stray far from the provincial history of one nation to learn that armies sometimes give laws to majorities. The epics of this hemisphere, to say nothing of ancient Greek travails, show how easily coups d'état can make black-mailing minorities despots.

In the American twentieth century, desperate minorities, lacking the power to bring off revolution, have characteristically opted for nonviolent resistance or nihilistic riot. But if armed might ever again becomes sufficiently uncertain while a minority becomes sufficiently rank, Americans may rediscover from personal experience why democracies sometimes collapse. An obsessed minority of a minority may again demand that the majority obey the minority. The majority may again insist with war or yield with self-loathing. A Jackson and a Calhoun may again experiment with an appeasement. But the conflict between an extremist's drive to live and a majority's drive to govern may prove beyond appeasement. In that case, arrogant Americans will soon enough again be humiliated by their armies.

A saving humility can come more painlessly from recapturing nineteenth-century history. The American Civil War, the most savage in history, makes the illusion that republics always work unpardonable conceit. Republics provide peaceful government only so long as men choose to accept decisions at the ballot box. Blackmail, whether it be called nullification or secession, is but a symptom that willingness to obey majorities no longer characterizes a minority. Democratic moralists can then waste their breath pronouncing blackmailers depraved. Extremists will answer that self-preservation is the first commandment of human existence. The answer signals that government has lost its communal foundation. The only question left is when the uprooted republic will topple.

ERIC FONER

Politics,
Ideology, and the Origins
of the American Civil War

I T HAS LONG BEEN AN AXIOM of political science that political
parties help to hold together diverse, heterogeneous societies like
our own. Since most major parties in American history have tried,
in Seymour Lipset's phrase, to "appear as plausible representatives
of the whole society," they have been broad coalitions cutting
across lines of class, race, religion, and section. And although party
competition requires that there be differences between the major
parties, these differences usually have not been along sharp ideological lines. In fact, the very diversity of American society has inhibited the formation of ideological parties, for such parties assume
the existence of a single line of social division along which a majority of the electorate can be mobilized. In a large, heterogeneous
society, such a line rarely exists. There are, therefore, strong reasons
why, in a two-party system, a major party—or a party aspiring to
become "major"—will eschew ideology, for the statement of a coherent ideology will set limits to the groups in the electorate the
party can hope to mobilize. Under most circumstances, in other
words, the party's role as a carrier of a coherent ideology will con-

flict with its role as an electoral machine bent on winning the widest possible number of votes.[1]

For much of the seventy years preceding the Civil War, the American political system functioned as a mechanism for relieving social tensions, ordering group conflict, and integrating the society. The existence of national political parties, increasingly focused on the contest for the Presidency, necessitated alliances between political elites in various sections of the country. A recent study of early American politics notes that "political nationalization was far ahead of economic, cultural, and social nationalization"—that is, that the national political system was itself a major bond of union in a diverse, growing society.[2] But as North and South increasingly took different paths of economic and social development and as, from the 1830's onwards, antagonistic value systems and ideologies grounded in the question of slavery emerged in these sections, the political system inevitably came under severe disruptive pressures. Because they brought into play basic values and moral judgments, the competing sectional ideologies could not be defused by the normal processes of political compromise, nor could they be contained within the existing inter-sectional political system. Once parties began to reorient themselves on sectional lines, a fundamental necessity of democratic politics—that each party look upon the other as a legitimate alternative government—was destroyed.

When we consider the causes of the sectional conflict, we must ask ourselves not only why civil war came when it did, but why it did not come sooner. How did a divided nation manage to hold itself together for as long as it did? In part, the answer lies in the unifying effects of inter-sectional political parties. On the level of politics, the coming of the Civil War is the story of the intrusion of sectional ideology into the political system, despite the efforts of political leaders of both parties to keep it out. Once this happened, political competition worked to exacerbate, rather than to solve, social and sectional conflicts. For as Frank Sorauf has explained:[3]

[1] Seymour M. Lipset, *The First New Nation* (New York, 1963), pp. 308-11; Frank J. Sorauf, *Political Parties in the American System* (Boston, 1964), pp. 60-65. Distinctions between American political parties, to borrow Marvin Meyers' apt phrase, have usually been along lines of "persuasion," rather than ideology.

[2] Donald L. Robinson, *Slavery and the Structure of American Politics 1765-1820* (New York, 1971), p. 175. See also William N. Chambers and Walter Dean Burham, eds., *The American Party Systems* (New York, 1967), pp. 3-32, 56-89.

[3] Sorauf, *Political Parties*, p. 61.

The party of extensive ideology develops in and reflects the society in which little consensus prevails on basic social values and institutions. It betokens deep social disagreements and conflicts. Indeed, the party of ideology that is also a major, competitive party accompanies a politics of almost total concern. Since its ideology defines political issues as including almost every facet of life, it brings to the political system almost every division, every difference, every conflict of any importance in society.

"Parties in this country," wrote a conservative northern Whig in 1855, "heretofore have helped, not delayed, the slow and difficult growth of a consummated nationality." Rufus Choate was lamenting the passing of a bygone era, a time when "our allies were everywhere . . . there were no Alleghenies nor Mississippi rivers in our politics."[4] Party organization and the nature of political conflict had taken on new and unprecedented forms in the 1850's. It is no accident that the break up of the last major inter-sectional party preceded by less than a year the break up of the Union or that the final crisis was precipitated not by any "overt act," but by a presidential election.

From the beginning of national government, of course, differences of opinion over slavery consituted an important obstacle to the formation of a national community. "The great danger to our general government," as Madison remarked at the Constitutional Convention, "is the great southern and northern interests of the continent, being opposed to each other." "The institution of slavery and its consequences," according to him, was the main "line of discrimination" in convention disputes. As far as slavery was concerned, the Constitution amply fulfilled Lord Acton's dictum that it was an effort to avoid settling basic questions. Aside from the Atlantic slave trade, Congress was given no power to regulate slavery in any way—the framers' main intention seems to have been to place slavery completely outside the national political arena. The only basis on which a national politics could exist—the avoidance of sectional issues—was thus defined at the outset.[5]

Although the slavery question was never completely excluded from political debate in the 1790's, and there was considerable Federalist grumbling about the three-fifths clause of the Constitution after 1800, the first full demonstration of the political

[4] *National Intelligencer*, October 6, 1855.

[5] Staughton Lynd, *Class Conflict, Slavery, and the United~States Constitution* (Indianapolis, 1967), p. 161; Robinson, *Slavery and the Structure of Politics* pp. viii, 244.

possibilities inherent in a sectional attack on slavery occurred in the Missouri controversy of 1819-21. These debates established a number of precedents which forecast the future course of the slavery extension issue in Congress. Most important was the fact that the issue was able for a time to completely obliterate party lines. In the first votes on slavery in Missouri, virtually every northerner, regardless of party, voted against expansion. It was not surprising, of course, that northern Federalists would try to make political capital out of the issue. What was unexpected was that northern Republicans, many of whom were aggrieved by Virginia's long dominance of the Presidency and by the Monroe administration's tariff and internal improvements policies, would unite with the Federalists. As John Quincy Adams observed, the debate "disclosed a secret: it revealed the basis for a new organization of parties . . . . Here was a new party really formed . . . terrible to the whole Union, but portentously terrible to the South." But the final compromise set another important precedent: enough northern Republicans became convinced that the Federalists were making political gains from the debates and that the Union was seriously endangered to break with the sectional bloc and support a compromise which a majority of northern Congressmen—Republicans and Federalists—opposed. As for the Monroe administration, its semiofficial spokesman, the *National Intelligencer*, pleaded for a return to the policy of avoiding sectional issues, even to the extent of refusing to publish letters which dealt in any way with the subject of slavery.[6]

The Missouri controversy and the election of 1824, in which four candidates contested the Presidency, largely drawing support from their home sections, revealed that in the absence of two-party competition, sectional loyalties would constitute the lines of political division. No one recognized this more clearly than the architect of the second-party system, Martin Van Buren. In his well-known letter to Thomas Ritchie of Virginia, Van Buren explained the need for a revival of national two-party politics on precisely this ground: "Party attachment in former times furnished a complete antidote for sectional prejudices by producing counteracting feelings. It was not until that defense had been

<hr/>

[6] James M. Banner, *To the Hartford Convention* (New York, 1970), pp. 99-103; Glover Moore, *The Missouri Controversy 1819-1821* (Lexington, Ky., 1953), *passim*; Charles Francis Adams, ed., *Memoirs of John Quincy Adams* (12 vols; Philadelphia, 1874-77), vol. IV, p. 529; William E. Ames, *A History of the National Intelligencer* (Chapel Hill, N.C., 1972), pp. 121-22.

broken down that the clamor against Southern Influence and African Slavery could be made effectual in the North." Van Buren and many of his generation of politicians had been genuinely frightened by the threats of disunion which echoed through Congress in 1820; they saw national two-party competition as the alternative to sectional conflict and eventual disunion. Ironically, as Richard McCormick has made clear, the creation of the second party system owed as much to sectionalism as to national loyalties. The South, for example, only developed an organized, competitive Whig party in 1835 and 1836 when it became apparent that Jackson, the southern President, had chosen Van Buren, a northerner, as his successor. Once party divisions had emerged, however, they stuck, and by 1840, for one of the very few times in American history, two truly inter-sectional parties, each united behind a single candidate, competed for the Presidency.[7]

The 1830's witnessed a vast expansion of political loyalties and awareness and the creation of party mechanisms to channel voter participation in politics. But the new mass sense of identification with politics had ominous implications for the sectional antagonisms which the party system sought to suppress. The historian of the Missouri Compromise has observed that "if there had been a civil war in 1819-1821 it would have been between the members of Congress, with the rest of the country looking on in amazement." This is only one example of the intellectual and political isolation of Washington from the general populace which James Young has described in *The Washington Community*.[8] The mass, non-ideological politics of the Jackson era created the desperately needed link between governors and governed. But this very link made possible the emergence of two kinds of sectional agitators: the abolitionists, who stood outside of politics and hoped to force public opinion—and through it, politicians—to confront the slavery issue, and political agitators, who used politics as a way of

[7]Paul Nagel, "The Election of 1824: Reconsideration Based on Newspaper Opinion," *Journal of Southern History* XXVI (1960), pp. 315-29; Richard H. Brown, "The Missouri Crisis, Slavery, and the Politics of Jacksonianism," *South Atlantic Quarterly* LXV (Winter 1966), pp. 55-72; Robert V. Remini, *Martin Van Buren and the Making of the Democratic Party* (New York, 1959), pp. 125-32; Richard P. McCormick, *The Second American Party System* (Chapel Hill, 1966), pp. 338-42; Chambers and Burnham, eds., *The American Party Systems*, pp. 21, 97-101.

[8]Moore, *Missouri Controversy*, p. 175; James Young, *The Washington Community* (New York, 1966).

heightening sectional self-consciousness and antagonism in the
populace at large.

Because of the rise of mass politics and the emergence of these
sectional agitators, the 1830's was the decade in which long-stand-
ing, latent sectional divisions were suddenly activated, and previously unrelated patterns of derogatory sectional imagery began
to emerge into full-blown sectional ideology. Many of the antislavery arguments which gained wide currency in the 1830's had
roots stretching back into the eighteenth century. The idea that
slavery degraded white labor and retarded economic development,
for example, had been voiced by Benjamin Franklin. After 1800,
the Federalists, increasingly localized in New England, had developed a fairly coherent critique, not only of the social and
economic effects of slavery, but of what Harrison Gray Otis called
the divergence of "manners, habits, customs, principles, and ways
of thinking" which separated northerners and southerners. And,
during the Missouri debates, almost every economic, political, and
moral argument against slavery that would be used in the later
sectional debate was voiced. In fact, one recurring argument was
not picked up later—the warning of northern Congressmen
that the South faced the danger of slave rebellion if steps were not
taken toward abolition. (As far as I know, only Thaddeus Stevens
of Republican spokesmen in the 1850's would explicitly use this
line of argument.)[9]

The similarity between Federalist attacks on the South and later
abolitionist and Republican arguments, coupled with the fact that
many abolitionists—including Garrison, Phillips, the Tappans, and
others—came from Federalist backgrounds, has led James Banner
to describe abolitionism as "the Massachusetts Federalist ideology
come back to life." Yet there was a long road to be travelled from
Harrison Gray Otis to William H. Seward, just as there was from
Thomas Jefferson to George Fitzhugh. For one thing, the Federalist distrust of democracy, social competition, the Jeffersonian cry
of "equal rights," their commitment to social inequality, hier-
archy, tradition, and order prevented them from pushing their

[9] Robinson, *Slavery and the Structure of Politics*, p. 72; Linda K. Kerber, *Federalists
in Dissent* (Ithaca, N.Y., 1970), pp. 24-44; Banner, *To the Hartford Convention*, pp.
104-9; Theophilus Parsons, Jr., "A Mirror of Mens' Minds: The Missouri Compromise
and the Development of an Antislavery Ideology," (unpublished seminar paper, Columbia University, 1971); *Congressional Globe*, 31 Congress, 1 Session, Appendix, p. 1030;
36 Congress, 2 Session, p. 624.C Vann Woodward has recently made the point that
patterns of derogatory sectional imagery existed far earlier than most historians have
assumed. Woodward, *American Counterpoint* (Boston, 1971), p. 6.

antislavery views to their logical conclusion. And New England Federalists were inhibited by the requirements of national party organization and competition from voicing antislavery views. In the 1790's, they maintained close ties with southern Federalists, and after 1800 hope of reviving their strength in the South never completely died. Only a party which embraced social mobility and competitive individualism, rejected the permanent subordination of any "rank" in society, and was unburdened by a southern wing could develop a fully coherent antislavery ideology.[10]

An equally important reason why the Federalists did not develop a consistent sectional ideology was that the South in the early part of the nineteenth century shared many of the Federalists' reservations about slavery. The growth of an antislavery ideology, in other words, depended in large measure on the growth of proslavery thought, and, by the same token, it was the abolitionist assault which brought into being the coherent defense of slavery. The opening years of the 1830's, of course, were ones of crisis for the South. The emergence of militant abolitionism, Nat Turner's rebellion, the Virginia debates on slavery, and the nullification crisis suddenly presented assaults to the institution of slavery from within and outside the South. The reaction was the closing of southern society in defense of slavery, "the most thorough-going repression of free thought, free speech, and a free press ever witnessed in an American community." At the same time, southerners increasingly abandoned their previous, highly qualified defenses of slavery and embarked on the formulation of the proslavery argument. By 1837, as is well known, John C. Calhoun could thank the abolitionists on precisely this ground:[11]

This agitation has produced one happy effect at least; it has compelled us at the South to look into the nature and character of this great institution, and to correct many false impressions that even we had entertained in relation to it. Many in the South once believed that it was a moral and political evil; that folly and delusion are gone; we see it now in its true light, and regard it as the most safe and stable basis for free institutions in the world.

[10] Banner, *To the Hartford Convention*, pp. 108-9; Kerber, *Federalists in Dissent* pp. 50, 59-63. After the transformation of their party from a national to a regional one, New England Federalists did express their latent anti-southern feelings more openly. Richard Buel, Jr., *Securing the Revolution: Ideology in American Politics, 1789-1815* (Ithaca, N.Y., 1972) p. 235.

[11] Stanley Elkins, "Slavery and Ideology," in Ann Lane, ed., *The Debate over Slavery* (Urbana, Ill., 1971), p. 376n.; William W. Freehling, *Prelude to Civil War*, (New York, 1966), ch. 9, esp. pp. 333, 358; *Congressional Globe*, 25 Congress, 2 Session, Appendix, p. 62.

The South, of course, was hardly as united as Calhoun asserted. But the progressive rejection of the Jeffersonian tradition, the suppression of civil liberties, and the increasing stridency of the defense of slavery all pushed the South further and further out of the inter-sectional mainstream, setting it increasingly apart from the rest of the country. Coupled with the Gag Rule and the mobs which broke up abolitionist presses and meetings, the growth of proslavery thought was vital to a new antislavery formulation which emerged in the late 1830's and which had been absent from both the Federalist attacks on slavery and the Missouri debates—the idea of the slave power. The slave power replaced the three-fifths clause as the symbol of southern power, and it was a far more sophisticated and complex formulation. Abolitionists could now argue that slavery was not only morally repugnant, it was incompatible with the basic democratic values and liberties of white Americans. As one abolitionist declared, "We commenced the present struggle to obtain the freedom of the slave; we are compelled to continue it to preserve our own." In other words, a process of ideological expansion had begun, fed in large measure by the sequence of response and counter-response between the competing sectional outlooks.[12] Once this process had begun, it had an internal dynamic which made it extremely difficult to stop. This was especially true because of the emergence of agitators whose avowed purpose was to sharpen sectional conflict, polarize public opinion, and develop sectional ideologies to their logical extremes.

As the 1840's opened, most political leaders still clung to the traditional basis of politics, but the sectional, ideological political agitators formed growing minorities in each section. In the South, there was a small group of outright secessionists and a larger group, led by Calhoun, who were firmly committed to the Union but who viewed sectional organization and self-defense, not the traditional reliance on inter-sectional political parties, as the surest means of protecting southern interests within the Union. In the North, a small radical group gathered in Congress around John Quincy Adams and Congressmen like Joshua Giddings, William Slade, and Seth Gates—men who represented areas of the most intense abolitionist agitation and whose presence confirmed Garrison's belief that, once public opinion was aroused on the slavery

[12] Alice Felt Typer, *Freedom's Ferment* (New York, 1962 ed.), p. 511; Elkins, "Slavery and Ideology," pp. 374-77; Eric Foner, *Free Soil, Free Labor, Free Men* (New York, 1970), pp. 87-102.

issue, politicians would have to follow step. These radicals were determined to force slavery into every Congressional debate. They were continually frustrated but never suppressed, and the reelection of Giddings in 1842 after his censure and resignation from the House proved that in some districts party discipline was no longer able to control the slavery issue.[13]

The northern political agitators, both Congressmen and Liberty party leaders, also performed the function of developing and popularizing a political rhetoric, especially focused on fear of the slave power, which could be seized upon by traditional politicians and large masses of voters if slavery ever entered the center of political conflict.

In the 1840's, this is precisely what happened. As one politician later recalled, "Slavery upon which by common consent no party issue had been made was then obtruded upon the field of party action." It is significant that John Tyler and John C. Calhoun, the two men most responsible for this intrusion, were political outsiders, men without places in the national party structure. Both of their careers were blocked by the major parties but might be advanced if tied to the slavery question in the form of Texas annexation. Once introduced into politics, slavery was there to stay. The Wilmot Proviso, introduced in 1846, had precisely the same effect as the proposal two decades earlier to restrict slavery in Missouri—it completely fractured the major parties along sectional lines. As in 1820, opposition to the expansion of slavery became the way in which a diverse group of northerners expressed their various resentments against a southern-dominated administration. And, as in 1821, a small group of northern Democrats eventually broke with their section, reaffirmed their primary loyalty to the party, and joined with the South to kill the Proviso in 1847. In the same year, enough southerners rejected Calhoun's call for united sectional action to doom his personal and sectional ambitions.[14]

But the slavery extension debates of the 1840's had far greater effects on the political system than the Missouri controversy had had. Within each party, they created a significant group of

[13] Gilbert H. Barnes, *The Anti-Slavery Impulse* (New York, 1964 ed.), pp. 188-90, 195-97; James B. Stewart, *Joshua R. Giddings and the Tactics of the Radical Politics* (Cleveland, 1970), ch. 4.

[14] Preston King to Gideon Welles, September 16, 1858, Gideon Welles Papers, Library of Congress; Eric Foner, "The Wilmot Proviso Revisited," *Journal of American History* LVI (September 1969), pp. 262-70; Chaplain W. Morrison, *Democratic Politics and Sectionalism* (Chapel Hill, N.C., 1967), pp. 34-41.

sectional politicians—men whose careers were linked to the slavery question and who would therefore resist its exclusion from future politics. And in the North, the 1840's witnessed the expansion of sectional political rhetoric—as more and more northerners became familiar with the "aggressions" of the slave power and the need to resist them. At the same time, as antislavery ideas expanded, unpopular and divisive elements were weeded out, especially the old alliance of antislavery with demands for the rights of free blacks. Opposition to slavery was already coming to focus on its lowest common denominators—free soil, opposition to the slave power, and union.[15]

The political system reacted to the intrusion of the slavery question in the traditional ways. At first, it tried to suppress it. This is the meaning of the famous letters opposing the immediate annexation of Texas issued by Clay and Van Buren on the same spring day in 1844, probably after consultation on the subject. It was an agreement that slavery was too explosive a question for either party to try to take partisan advantage of it. The agreement, of course, was torpedoed by the defeat of Van Buren for the Democratic nomination, a defeat caused in part by the willingness of his Democratic opponents to use the Texas and slavery questions to discredit Van Buren—thereby violating the previously established rules of political conduct. In the North from 1844 onwards, both parties, particularly the Whigs, tried to defuse the slavery issue and minimize defection to the Liberty party by adopting anti-southern rhetoric. This tended to prevent defections to third parties, but it had the effect of nurturing and legitimating anti-southern sentiment within the ranks of the major parties themselves. After the 1848 election in which northern Whigs and Democrats vied for title of "free soil" to minimize the impact of the Free Soil party, William H. Seward commented, "Antislavery is at length a respectable element in politics."[16]

Both parties also attempted to devise formulas for compromising the divisive issue. For the Whigs, it was "no territory"—an end to expansion would end the question of the spread of slavery. The Democratic answer, first announced by Vice President Dallas in

[15] Morrison, *Democratic Politics*, pp. 45-51; Eric Foner, "Racial Attitudes of the New York Free Soilers," *New York History* XLVI (October 1965), pp. 311-29.

[16] Avery Craven, *The Coming of the Civil War* (Chicago, 1942), p. 197; Ronald P. Formisano, *The Birth of Mass Political Parties* (Princeton, N.J., 1971), pp. 195, 205-6; Joseph G. Rayback, *Free Soil* (Lexington, 1970), p. 309; Frederick W. Seward, *Seward at Washington* (New York 1891), vol. I, p. 71.

1847 and picked up by Lewis Cass, was popular sovereignty or nonintervention: giving to the people of each territory the right to decide on slavery. As has often been pointed out, popular sovereignty was an exceedingly vague and ambiguous doctrine. It was never precisely clear what the powers of a territorial legislature were to be or at what point the question of slavery was to be decided.[17] But politically such ambiguity was essential (and intentional) if popular sovereignty were to serve as a means of settling the slavery issue on the traditional basis—by removing it from national politics and transferring the battleground from Congress to the territories.[18] Popular sovereignty formed one basis of the compromise of 1850, the last attempt of the political system to expel the disease of sectional ideology by finally settling all the points at which slavery and national politics intersected.

That compromise was possible in 1850 was testimony to the resiliency of the political system and the continuing ability of party loyalty to compete with sectional commitments. But the very method of passage revealed how deeply sectional divisions were embedded in party politics. Because only a small group of Congressmen—mostly northwestern Democrats and southern Whigs—were committed to compromise on every issue, the "omnibus" compromise measure could not pass. The compromise had to be enacted serially with the small compromise bloc, led by Stephen A. Douglas of Illinois, aligned with first one sectional bloc, then the other, to pass the individual measures.[19]

His role in the passage of the compromise announced the emergence of Douglas as the last of the great Unionist, compromising politicians, the heir of Clay, Webster, and other spokesmen for the center. And his career, like Webster's, showed that it was no longer possible to win the confidence of both sections with a combination of extreme nationalism and the calculated suppression of the slavery issue in national politics. Like his predecessors, Douglas called for a policy of "entire silence on the slavery question," and throughout the 1850's, as Robert Johannsen has written, his aim was to restore "order and stability to American politics through the agency of a national, conserva-

[17] Foner, *Free Soil, Free Labor, Free Men*, p. 188; Morrison, *Democratic Politics*, pp. 87-91; Damon Wells, *Stephen Douglas, The Last Years, 1857-1861* (Austin, Tex., 1971) pp. 61-67.

[18] For the intentional nature of the ambiguities in popular sovereignty, see Robert W. Johannsen, *Stephen A. Douglas* (New York, 1973), pp. 427, 440, 525.

[19] Holman Hamilton, *Prologue to Conflict* (Lexington, Ky., 1964).

tive Democratic party." Ultimately, Douglas failed—a traditional career for the Union was simply not possible in the 1850's—but it is equally true that in 1860 he was the only presidential candidate to draw significant support in all parts of the country.[20]

It is, of course, highly ironic that it was Douglas' attempt to extend the principle of popular sovereignty to territory already guaranteed to free labor by the Missouri Compromise which finally shattered the second-party system. We can date almost exactly the final collapse of that system—February 15, 1854—the day a caucus of southern Whig Congressmen and Senators decided to support Douglas' Nebraska bill, despite the fact that they could have united with northern Whigs in opposition both to the repeal of the Missouri Compromise and the revival of sectional agitation.[21] But in spite of the sectionalization of politics which occurred after 1854, Douglas continued his attempt to maintain a national basis of party competition. In fact, from one angle of vision, whether politics was to be national or sectional was the basic issue of the Lincoln-Douglas debates of 1858. The Little Giant presented local autonomy—popular sovereignty for states and territories—as the only "national" solution to the slavery question, while Lincoln attempted to destroy this middle ground and force a single, sectional solution on the entire Union. There is a common critique of Douglas' politics, expressed perhaps most persuasively by Allan Nevins, which argues that, as a man with no moral feelings about slavery, Douglas was incapable of recognizing that this moral issue affected millions of northern voters.[22] This, in my opinion, is a serious misunderstanding of Douglas' politics. What he insisted was not that there was no moral question involved in slavery but that it was not the function of the politician to deal in moral judgments. To Lincoln's prediction that the nation could not exist half slave and half free, Douglas replied that it had so existed for seventy years and could continue to do so if northerners stopped trying to impose their own brand of morality upon the South.

[20] Johannsen, *Douglas*, pp. 347, 483. For Webster's efforts to create a national consensus by compromising and suppressing the slavery issue, see Robert F. Dalzell, Jr., *Daniel Webster and the Trial of American Nationalism* (Boston, 1973), *passim*, and Major L. Wilson, "Of Time and the Union: Webster and His Critics in the Crisis of 1850," *Civil War History* XIV (December 1968), pp. 293-306.

[21] Foner, *Free Soil, Free Labor, Free Men*, p. 194. Of course, on the local level, the Whigs had already been eroding under the impact of such divisive issues as temperance and nativism.

[22] Allan Nevins, *Ordeal of the Union* (New York, 1947), vol. II, p. 107. Cf. Wells, *Douglas*, p. 64.

Douglas' insistence on the separation of politics and morality was expressed in his oft-quoted statement that—in his role as a politician—he did not care if the people of a territory voted slavery "up or down." As he explained in his Chicago speech of July, 1858, just before the opening of the great debates:

I deny the right of Congress to force a slave-holding state upon an unwilling people. I deny their right to force a free state upon an unwilling people. I deny their right to force a good thing upon a people who are unwilling to receive it. . . . It is no answer to this argument to say that slavery is an evil and hence should not be tolerated. You must allow the people to decide for themselves whether it is a good or an evil.

When Lincoln, therefore, said the real purpose of popular sovereignty was "to educate and mould public opinion, at least northern public opinion, to not care whether slavery is voted down or up," he was, of course, right. For Douglas recognized that moral categories, being essentially uncompromisable, are unassimilable in politics. The only solution to the slavery issue was local autonomy. Whatever a majority of a state or territory wished to do about slavery was right—or at least should not be tampered with by politicians from other areas. To this, Lincoln's only possible reply was the one formulated in the debates—the will of the majority must be tempered by considerations of morality. Slavery was not, he declared, an "*ordinary* matter of domestic concern in the states and territories." Because of its essential immorality, it tainted the entire nation, and its disposition in the territories, and eventually in the entire nation, was a matter of national concern to be decided by a national, not a local, majority. As the debates continued, Lincoln increasingly moved to this moral level of the slavery argument: "Everything that emanates from [Douglas] or his coadjutors, carefully excludes the thought that there is anything wrong with slavery. All their arguments, if you will consider them, will be seen to exclude the thought . . . . If you do admit that it is wrong, Judge Douglas can't logically say that he don't care whether a wrong is voted up or down."[23]

In order to press home the moral argument, moreover, Lincoln had to insist throughout the debates on the basic humanity of the black; while Douglas, by the same token, logically had to define

[23] Paul M. Angle, ed., *Created Equal? The Complete Lincoln-Douglas Debates of 1858* (Chicago, 1958), pp. 5, 17, 18, 35, 70, 202, 303, 332-34, 351. Cf. Harry Jaffa, *Crisis of the House Divided* (Garden City, N.J., 1959); Wells, *Douglas*, pp. 110-11.

blacks as subhuman, or at least, as the Dred Scott decision had
insisted, not part of the American "people" included in the
Declaration of Independence and the Constitution. Douglas' view
of the black, Lincoln declared, conveyed "no vivid impression that
the Negro is a human, and consequently has no idea that there can
be any moral question in legislating about him."[24] Of course, the
standard of morality which Lincoln felt the nation should adopt
regarding slavery and the black was the sectional morality of the
Republican party.

By 1860, Douglas' local majoritarianism was no more acceptable to southern political leaders than Lincoln's national and
moral majoritarianism. The principle of state rights and minority
self-determination had always been the first line of defense of
slavery from northern interference, but southerners now coupled
it with the demand that Congress intervene to establish and
guarantee slavery in the territories. The Lecompton fight had clearly demonstrated that southerners would no longer be satisfied with
what Douglas hoped the territories would become—free, Democratic states. And the refusal of the Douglas Democrats to accede
to southern demands was the culmination of a long history of
resentment on the part of northern Democrats, stretching back
into the 1840's, at the impossible political dilemma of being
caught between increasingly anti-southern constituency pressure
and loyalty to an increasingly pro-southern national party. For
their part, southern Democrats viewed their northern allies as too
weak at home and too tainted with anti-southernism after the
Lecompton battle to be relied on to protect southern interests
any longer.[25]

----

[24] Angle, ed., *Created Equal?* pp. 22-23, 62-63; Jaffa, *Crisis*, 36. Lincoln declared
that the trouble with popular sovereignty was that Douglas "looks upon all this matter
of slavery as an exceedingly little thing—this matter of keeping one-sixth of the
population of the whole country in a state of oppression and tyranny unequalled in the
world." Angle, ed., *Created Equal?* p. 35. It is hard to imagine Douglas including the
slaves in any way as part of "the population of the whole country."

[25] Roy F. Nichols, *The Disruption of American Democracy* (New York, 1948), esp.
ch. 15. For Douglas' intentions for the territories and his expectation that popular
sovereignty would result in the creation of free states in the West, see Jaffa, *Crisis*, p. 48;
Johannsen, *Douglas*, pp. 276, 279-80, 565; Edward L. and Frederick H. Schapsmeir,
"Lincoln and Douglas: Their Versions of the West," *Journal of the West* VII (October
1968), p. 546. Lee Benson argues that the entrance of free western states into the Union
was not a cause of concern for the South, since these new states, like California and
Oregon in the 1850's, would likely be Democratic and pro-southern. But the 1850's
clearly showed that free, Democratic states could quickly become Republican, and the
Lecompton fight demonstrated that free, Democratic states were no longer acceptable to
southern leaders, who insisted that Kansas be Democratic *and* slave. Lee Benson, *Toward
the Scientific Study of History* (Philadelphia, 1972), p. 269.

As for the Republicans, by the late 1850's they had succeeded in developing a coherent ideology which, despite internal ambiguities and contradictions, incorporated the fundamental values, hopes, and fears of a majority of northerners. As I have argued elsewhere, it rested on a commitment to the northern social order, founded on the dignity and opportunities of free labor, and to social mobility, enterprise, and "progress." It gloried in the same qualities of northern life—materialism, social fluidity, and the dominance of the self-made man—which twenty years earlier had been the source of widespread anxiety and fear in Jacksonian America. And it defined the South as a backward, stagnant, aristocratic society, totally alien in values and social order to the middle-class capitalism of the North.[26]

Some elements of the Republican ideology had roots stretching back into the eighteenth century. Others, especially the Republican emphasis on the threat of the slave power, were relatively new. Northern politics and thought were permeated by the slave power idea in the 1850's. The effect can perhaps be gauged by a brief look at the career of the leading Republican spokesman of the 1850's, William H. Seward. As a political child of upstate New York's burned-over district and anti-masonic crusade, Seward had long believed that the Whig party's main political liability was its image as the spokeman of the wealthy and aristocratic. Firmly committed to egalitarian democracy, Seward had attempted to reorient the New York State Whigs into a reformist, egalitarian party, friendly to immigrants and embracing political and economic democracy, but he was always defeated by the party's downstate conservative wing. In the 1840's, he became convinced that the only way for the party to counteract the Democrats' monopoly of the rhetoric of democracy and equality was for the Whigs to embrace antislavery as a party platform.[27]

The slave power idea gave the Republicans the anti-aristocratic appeal with which men like Seward had long wished to be associated politically. By fusing older antislavery arguments with the idea that slavery posed a threat to northern free labor and democratic values, it enabled the Republicans to tap the egalitar-

[26] Foner, *Free Soil, Free Labor, Free Men*, esp. chs. 1-2.

[27] Glyndon G. Van Deusen, *William Henry Seward* (New York, 1969), ch. 9; Elliot R. Barkan, "The Emergence of a Whig Persuasion: Conservatism, Democratism, and the New York State Whigs," *New York History* LII (October 1971), pp. 370-86; Seward to James Bowen, November 3, 1844, Seward Papers, University of Michigan Library; Seward to Weed, August 3, 1846, Thurlow Weed Papers, University of Rochester Library.

ian outlook which lay at the heart of northern society. At the same time, it enabled Republicans to present antislavery as an essentially conservative reform, an attempt to reestablish the antislavery principles of the founding fathers and rescue the federal government from southern usurpation. And, of course, the slave power idea had a far greater appeal to northern self-interest than arguments based on the plight of black slaves in the South. As the black abolitionist Frederick Douglass noted, "The cry of Free Men was raised, not for the extension of liberty to the black man, but for the protection of the liberty of the white."[28]

By the late 1850's, it had become a standard part of Republican rhetoric to accuse the slave power of a long series of transgressions against northern rights and liberties and to predict that, unless halted by effective political action, the ultimate aim of the conspiracy—the complete subordination of the national government to slavery and the suppression of northern liberties—would be accomplished. Like other conspiracy theories, the slave power idea was a way of ordering and interpreting history, assigning clear causes to otherwise inexplicable events, from the Gag Rule to Bleeding Kansas and the Dred Scott decision. It also provided a convenient symbol through which a host of anxieties about the future could be expressed. At the same time, the notion of a black Republican conspiracy to overthrow slavery and southern society had taken hold in the south. These competing conspiratorial outlooks were reflections, not merely of sectional "paranoia," but of the fact that the nation was every day growing apart and into two societies whose ultimate interests were diametrically opposed. The South's fear of black Republicans, despite its exaggerated rhetoric, was based on the realistic assessment that at the heart of Republican aspirations for the nation's future was the restriction and eventual eradication of slavery. And the slave power expressed northerners' conviction, not only that slavery was incompatible with basic democratic values, but that to protect slavery, southerners were determined to control the federal government and use it to foster the expansion of slavery. In summary, the slave power idea was the ideological glue of the Republican party—it enabled them to elect in 1860 a man conservative enough to sweep to victory in every northern state, yet radical enough to trigger the secession crisis.

[28] Formisano, *Birth of Mass Political Parties*, p. 329; Foner, *Free Soil, Free Labor, Free Men*, pp. 87-102; Larry Gara, "Slavery and the Slave Power: A Crucial Distinction," *Civil War History* XV (March 1969), pp. 5-18.

Did the election of Lincoln pose any real danger to the institution of slavery? In my view, it is only possible to argue that it did not if one takes a completely static—and therefore ahistorical—view of the slavery issue. The expansion of slavery was not simply an issue; it was a fact. By 1860, over half the slaves lived in areas outside the original slave states. At the same time, however, the South had become a permanent and shrinking minority within the nation. And in the majority section, antislavery sentiment had expanded at a phenomenal rate. Within one generation, it had moved from the commitment of a small minority of northerners to the motive force behind a victorious party. That sentiment now demanded the exclusion of slavery from the territories. Who could tell what its demands would be in ten or twenty years? The incoming President had often declared his commitment to the "ultimate extinction" of slavery. In Alton, Illinois, in the heart of the most proslavery area of the North, he had condemned Douglas because "he looks to no end of the institution of slavery."[29] A Lincoln administration seemed likely to be only the beginning of a prolonged period of Republican hegemony. And the succession of generally weak, one-term Presidents between 1836 and 1860 did not obscure the great expansion in the potential power of the presidency which had taken place during the administration of Andrew Jackson. Old Hickory had clearly shown that a strong-willed President, backed by a united political party, had tremendous power to shape the affairs of government and to transform into policy his version of majority will.

What was at stake in 1860, as in the entire sectional conflict, was the character of the nation's future. This was one reason Republicans had placed so much stress on the question of the expansion of slavery. Not only was this the most available issue concerning slavery constitutionally open to them, but it involved the nation's future in the most direct way. In the West, the future was tabula rasa, and the future course of western development

---

[29] Angle, ed., *Created Equal?* p. 393. It is futile, in my opinion, to draw too-fine distinctions between various kinds of Republican antislavery sentiment, as Lee Benson and Ronald Formisano sometimes have a tendency to do. Though the distinctions between opposition to the slave power, general anti-southernism, and what Formisano calls criticisms of "slavery as an institution," or "antislavery as such" were real ones, these distinctions seemed pointless to the South, since even Republicans of the most moderate antislavery views advocated policies southerners found unacceptable. More important, the varying degrees and kinds of antislavery sentiment fed into and reinforced one another; the Rupublican ideology, in other words, was much more than the sum of its parts—it must be understood in its totality. See Formisano, *Birth of Mass Political Parties*, pp. 244, 279; Benson, *Toward the Scientific Study*, p. 295.

would gravely affect the direction of the entire nation. Now that the territorial issue was settled by Lincoln's election, it seemed likely that the slavery controversy would be transferred back into the southern states themselves. Secessionists, as William Freehling has argued, feared that slavery was weak and vulnerable in the border states, even in Virginia.[30] They feared Republican efforts to encourage the formation of Republican organizations in these areas and the renewal of the long-suppressed internal debate on slavery in the South itself. And, lurking behind these anxieties, may have been fear of antislavery debate reaching the slave quarters, of an undermining of the masters' authority, and, ultimately, of slave rebellion itself. The slaveholders knew, despite the great economic strength of King Cotton, that the existence of slavery as a local institution in a larger free economy demanded an inter-sectional community consensus, real or enforced. It was this consensus which Lincoln's election seemed to undermine, which is why the secession convention of South Carolina declared, "Experience has proved that slaveholding states cannot be safe in subjection to non-slaveholding states."[31]

More than seventy years before the secession crisis, James Madison had laid down the principles by which a central government and individual and minority liberties could coexist in a large and heterogeneous Union. The very diversity of interests in the nation, he argued in the Federalist papers, was the security for the rights of minorities, for it ensured that no one interest would ever gain control of the government.[32] In the 1830's, John C. Calhoun recognized the danger which abolitionism posed to the South—it threatened to rally the North in the way Madison had said would not happen—in terms of one commitment hostile to the interests of the minority South. Moreover, Calhoun recognized, when a majority interest is organized into an effective political party, it can seize control of all the branches of government,

[30] William W. Freehling, "The Editorial Revolution, Virginia, and the Coming of the Civil War: A Review Essay," *Civil War History XVI* (March 1970), pp. 68-71.

[31] Robert Brent Toplin, "The Specter of Crisis: Slaveholder Reactions to Abolitionism in the United States and Brazil," *Civil War History* XVIII (June 1972), pp. 129-38; John Amasa May and Joan Reynolds Faust, *South Carolina Secedes* (Columbia, 1960), p. 88.

[32] Benjamin F. Wright, ed., *The Federalist* (Cambridge, 1961), pp. 132-34, 357-59. Or, as C. B. MacPherson writes, the American federal theory of politics rests on the assumption "that the politically important demands of each individual are diverse and are shared with varied and shifting combinations of other individuals, none of which combinations can be expected to be a numerical majority of the electorate." MacPherson, *Democratic Theory: Essays in Retrieval* (Oxford, 1973), p. 190.

overturning the system of constitutional checks and balances which supposedly protected minority rights. Only the principle of the concurrent majority—a veto which each major interest could exercise over policies directly affecting it—could reestablish this constitutional balance.

At the outset of the abolitionist crusade, Calhoun had been convinced that, while emancipation must be "resisted at all costs," the South should avoid hasty action until it was "certain that it is the real object, not by a few, but by a very large portion of the non-slaveholding states." By 1850, Calhoun was convinced that "Every portion of the North entertains views more or less hostile to slavery." And by 1860, the election returns demonstrated that this antislavery sentiment, contrary to Madison's expectations, had united in an interest capable of electing a President, despite the fact that it had not the slightest support from the sectional minority. The character of Lincoln's election, in other words, completely overturned the ground rules which were supposed to govern American politics. The South Carolina secession convention expressed secessionists' reaction when it declared that once the sectional Republican party, founded on hostility to southern values and interests, took over control of the federal government, "the guarantees of the Constitution will then no longer exist."[33]

Thus the South came face to face with a conflict between its loyalty to the nation and loyalty to the South—that is, to slavery, which, more than anything else, made the South distinct. David Potter has pointed out that the principle of majority rule implies the existence of a coherent, clearly recognizable body of which more than half may be legitimately considered as a majority of the whole. For the South to accept majority rule in 1860, in other words, would have been an affirmation of a common nationality with the North. Certainly, it is true that in terms of ethnicity, language, religion—many of the usual components of nationality— Americans, North and South, were still quite close. On the other hand, one important element, community of interest, was not present. And perhaps most important, the preceding decades had witnessed an escalation of distrust—an erosion of the reciprocal currents of good will so essential for national harmony. "We are not one peo-

---

[33] William W. Freehling, "Spoilsmen and Interests in the Thought and Career of John C. Calhoun," *Journal of American History* LII (June 1965), pp. 25-26; Charles M. Wiltse, *John C. Calhoun* (3 vols.; Indianapolis, 1944-51), vol. II, pp. 114, 195, 199, 255, 268-70; vol. III, pp. 416-19, 462-63; May and Faust, *South Carolina Secedes*, p. 81.

ple." declared the New York Tribune in 1855. "We are two peoples. We are a people for Freedom and a people for Slavery. Between the two, conflict is inevitable."[34] We can paraphrase John Adams' famous comment on the American Revolution and apply it to the coming of the Civil War—the separation was complete, in the minds of the people, before the war began. In a sense, the Constitution and national political system had failed in the difficult task of creating a nation—only the Civil War itself would accomplish it.

[34] David Potter, *The South and the Sectional Conflict* (Baton Rouge, 1968), pp. 44, 58; *New York Tribune*, April 12, 1855.

DON E. FEHRENBACHER

Only His Stepchildren:
Lincoln and the Negro

Ｉ F THE UNITED STATES had a patron saint, it would no doubt be Abraham Lincoln; and, if one undertook to explain Lincoln's extraordinary hold on the national consciousness, it would be difficult to find a better starting point than these lines from an undistinguished poem written in 1865.[1]

> One of the people! Born to be
> Their curious epitome;
> To share yet rise above
> Their shifting hate and love.

A man of the people and yet something much more, sharing popular passions and yet rising above them—here was the very ideal of a democratic leader, who in his person could somehow mute the natural antagonism between strong leadership and

This essay was presented at Gettysburg College, November 19, 1973, as the Twelfth Annual Robert Fortenbaugh Memorial Lecture, and at the College of William and Mary, November 28, 1973, as a James Pinckney Harrison Lecture. It appeared in the December 1974 issue of *Civil War History* and is published here by permission.

[1]Richard Henry Stoddard, *Abraham Lincoln: An Horation Ode*, cited in Roy P. Basler, *The Lincoln Legend: A Study in Changing Conceptions* (Boston, 1935), p. 234.

vigorous democracy. Amy Lowell, picking up the same theme half a century later, called Lincoln "an embodiment of the highest form of the typical American."[2] This paradox of the uncommon common man, splendidly heroic and at the same time appealingly representative, was by no means easy to sustain. The Lincoln tradition, as a consequence, came to embrace two distinct and seemingly incompatible legends—the awkward, amiable, robust, rail-splitting, story-telling, frontier folklore hero and the towering figure of the Great Emancipator and Savior of the Union, a man of sorrows, Christlike in his character and fate.

Biographers have struggled earnestly with this conspicuous dualism, but even when the excesses of reminiscence and myth are trimmed away, Lincoln remains a puzzling mixture of often conflicting qualities such as drollness and melancholy, warmth and reserve, skepticism and piety, humbleness and self-assurance. Furthermore, he is doubly hard to get at because he did not readily reveal his inner self. He left us no diary or memoirs, and his closest friends called him "secretive" and "shut-mouthed." Billy Herndon in one of his modest moods declared, "Lincoln is unknown and possibly always will be."[3] Plainly, there is good reason for scholarly caution in any effort to take the measure of such a man.

No less plain is the intimate connection between the Lincoln legend and the myth of America. The ambiguities in his popular image and the whisper of enigma in his portraits have probably broadened the appeal of this homespun westerner, self-made man, essential democrat, and national martyr. Almost anyone can find a way to identify with Lincoln, perhaps because "like Shakespear . . . he seemed to run through the whole gamut of human nature."[4] Whatever the complex of reasons, successive generations of his countrymen have accepted Abraham Lincoln as the consummate American—the representative genius of the nation. One consequence is that he tends to serve as a mirror for Americans, who, when they write about him, frequently divulge a good deal about themselves.

Of course the recurring election of Lincoln as *representative American* has never been unanimous. There was vehement dissent at first from many unreconstructed rebels and later from icono-

[2] *Ibid.*, pp. 264-65.

[3] David Donald, *Lincoln's Herndon* (New York, 1948), p. 305.

[4] John T. Morse, Jr., *Abraham Lincoln* (2 vols.; Boston, 1893), II, p. 355.

clasts such as Edgar Lee Masters and cavaliers of the Lost Cause such as Lyon Gardiner Tyler. In the mainstream of national life, however, it became increasingly fashionable for individuals and organizations to square themselves with Lincoln and enlist him in their enterprises. Often this required misquotation or misrepresentation or outright invention; but lobbyists and legislators, industrialists and labor leaders, reformers and bosses, Populists, Progressives, Prohibitionists, and Presidents all wanted him on their side. New Deal Democrats tried to steal him from the Republicans, and the American Communist Party bracketed him with Lenin. Lincoln, in the words of David Donald, had come to be "everybody's grandfather."[5]

Most remarkable of all was the growing recognition of Lincoln's greatness in the eleven states of the onetime Confederacy, ten of which had never given him a single vote for President. This may have been a necessary symbolic aspect of sectional reconciliation. Returning to the Union meant coming to terms with the man who had saved the Union. No one took the step more unequivocally than Henry W. Grady, prophet of the New South, who told a New York audience in 1886 that Lincoln had been "the first typical American, the first who comprehended within himself all the strength and gentleness, all the majesty and grace of this Republic."[6] When southerners talked to southerners about it, they were usually more restrained. Nevertheless, by the early twentieth century, the Lincoln tradition was becoming a blend of blue and gray, as illustrated in *The Perfect Tribute*, a story from the pen of an Alabama woman about a dying Confederate soldier's admiration for the Gettysburg Address.[7]

Bonds of sympathy between Lincoln and the South had not been difficult to find. He was, after all, a native southerner—implacable as an enemy but magnanimous in victory and compassionate by nature. In his hands, nearly everyone agreed, the ordeal of Reconstruction would have been less severe. Even Jefferson Davis concluded that his death had been "a great misfortune to the South."[8]

In addition, Lincoln seemed to pass the supreme test. He could be assimilated to the racial doctrines and institutional arrange-

[5] David Donald, *Lincoln Reconsidered* (2nd ed.; New York, 1969), p. 16.

[6] Michael Davis, *The Image of Lincoln in the South* (Knoxville, Tenn., 1971), p. 159.

[7] *Ibid.*, p. 138.

[8] *Ibid.*, p. 103.

ments associated with the era of segregation. The historical record, though not entirely consistent, indicated that his opposition to slavery had never included advocacy of racial equality. With a little editing here and some extra emphasis there, Lincoln came out "right" on the Negro question. This was a judgment more often understood than elaborated in southern writing and oratory, but certain self-appointed guardians of white supremacy were sometimes painfully explicit in claiming Lincoln as one of their own. He had been willing, they said, to guarantee slavery forever in the states where it already existed. He had issued the Emancipation Proclamation with great reluctance. He had opposed the extension of slavery only in order to reserve the Western territories exclusively for white men. He had denied favoring political and social equality for Negroes, had endorsed separation of the races, and had persistently recommended colonization of Negroes abroad. This was the Lincoln eulogized by James K. Vardaman of Mississippi, perhaps the most notorious political racist in American history, and by the sensational Negrophobic novelist Thomas Dixon. In his most famous work, *The Clansman*, Dixon had Lincoln as President parody himself during a discussion of colonization.

We can never attain the ideal Union our fathers dreamed, with millions of an alien, inferior race among us, whose assimilation is neither possible nor desirable. The Nation cannot now exist half white and half black, any more than it could exist half slave and half free.[9]

When one remembers that all this time millions of black Americans were still paying homage to the Great Emancipator, dualism begins to seem pervasive in the Lincoln tradition. Racist elements, to be sure, were never very successful in promoting the image of Lincoln as a dedicated white supremacist, but support from an unlikely quarter would eventually give the idea not only new life but respectability in the centers of professional scholarship.

During the first half of the twentieth century, Lincoln studies became a functional part of the literature of the Civil War, in which the problem of race was present but not paramount. Titles of the 1940's indicate the general bent of interest: *Lincoln and His Party in the Secession Crisis, Lincoln and the Patronage, Lincoln's*

[9]Thomas Dixon, *The Clansman: An Historical Romance of the Ku Klux Klan* (New York, 1905), p. 46; Davis, *Image*, pp. 147-52.

War Cabinet, Lincoln and the Radicals, Lincoln and the War Governors, Lincoln and the South. There was, it should be observed, no *Lincoln and the Negro.* That would come, appropriately, in the 1960's.

The sweep of the modern civil rights movement, beginning with the Supreme Court's anti-segregation decision in 1954, inspired a new departure in American historical writing. Never has the psychological need for a usable past been more evident. Black history flourished and so did abolitionist history, but the most prestigious field of endeavor was white-over-black history. Attention shifted, for example, from slavery as a cause of the Civil War to slavery as one major form of racial oppression. With this change of emphasis, the antebellum years began to look different. A number of monographs appearing in the 1960's, such as Leon F. Litwack's *North of Slavery*, demonstrated the nationwide prevalence of white-superiority doctrines and white-supremacy practices. Many Republicans and even some abolitionists, when they talked about the Negro, had sounded curiously like the slaveholders whom they were so fiercely denouncing. In fact, it appeared that the North and the South, while bitterly at odds on the issue of slavery, were relatively close to one another in their attitudes toward race. And Lincoln, according to Litwack, "accurately and consistently reflected the thoughts and prejudices of most Americans."[10]

The racial consensus of the Civil War era made it easy enough to understand why black Americans failed to win the equality implicit in emancipation, but certain other historical problems became more difficult as a consequence. For instance, if most northerners in 1860 were indeed racists who viewed the Negro with repugnance as an inferior order of creation, then why did so many of them have such strong feelings about slavery? And why did racist southerners fear and distrust racist Republicans with an intensity sufficient to destroy the Union? And does not the achievement of emancipation by a people so morally crippled with racism seem almost miraculous—like a one-armed man swimming the English Channel? No amount of talk about overwrought emotions or ulterior purposes or unintended consequences will fully account for what appears to be a major historical paradox, with Lincoln as the central figure.

[10]Leon F. Litwack, *North of Slavery: The Negro in the Free States, 1790-1860* (Chicago, 1961), p. 276.

When the civil rights struggle got under way in the 1950's, there were efforts on both sides to enlist Lincoln's support, but the primary tendency at first was to regard desegregation as a belated resumption of the good work begun with the Emancipation Proclamation. Many leading historians agreed that during the presidential years there had been a "steady evolution of Lincoln's attitude toward Negro rights."[11] The changes carried him a long way from the narrow environmental influences of his youth and made him, in the words of Richard N. Current, more relevant and inspiring than ever "as a symbol of man's ability to outgrow his prejudices."[12]

This was the liberal interpretation of Lincoln's record on racial matters. It came under attack from several directions but especially from the ranks of intellectual radicalism and black militancy, both academic and otherwise. New Left historians, many of them activists in the battle for racial justice, could find little to admire in Abraham Lincoln. Compared with abolitionists such as William Lloyd Garrison and Wendell Phillips, he seemed unheroic, opportunistic, and somewhat insensitive to the suffering of black people in bondage. He was "the prototype of the political man in power, with views so moderate as to require the pressure of radicals to stimulate action."[13] His prewar opposition to slavery, embracing the Republican policy of nonextension and the hope of ultimate extinction, reflected a "comfortable belief in the benevolence of history." It amounted to a "formula which promised in time to do everything while for the present risking nothing."[14]

Election to the Presidency, in the radical view, produced no great transformation of his character. "Lincoln grew during the war—but he didn't grow much," wrote Lerone Bennett, Jr., a senior editor of *Ebony*. "On every issue relating to the black man . . . he was the very essence of the white supremacist with good intentions."[15] He moved but slowly and reluctantly toward abolishing slavery, and his famous Proclamation not only lacked "moral grandeur" but had been drafted "in such a way that it

[11] Fawn M. Brodie, "Who Defends the Abolitonists?" *in* Martin Duberman, ed., *The Antislavery Vanguard: New Essays on the Abolitionists* (Princeton, N.J., 1965), pp. 63-64.

[12] Richard N. Current, *The Lincoln Nobody Knows* (New York, 1958), p. 236.

[13] Howard Zinn, "Abolitionists, Freedom-Riders, and the Tactics of Agitation," *in* Duberman, ed., *Antislavery Vanguard*, pp. 438-39.

[14] Martin Duberman, "The Northern Response to Slavery," in *ibid.*, pp. 396, 402.

[15] Lerone Bennett, Jr., "Was Abe Lincoln a White Supremacist?" *Ebony* XXIII (February 1968), p. 37.

freed few, if any, slaves."[16] His reputation as the Great Emancipator is therefore "pure myth."[17] Most important of all, Lincoln
probably believed in the inferiority of the Negro and certainly
favored separation of the races. He was, in Bennett's words, "a
tragically flawed figure who shared the racial prejudices of most
of his white contemporaries."[18]

This, then, was the radical interpretation of Lincoln's record on
racial matters, and what strikes one immediately is its similarity to
the views of professional racists like Vardaman and Dixon. The
portrait of A. Lincoln, Great White Supremacist, has been the
work, it seems, of a strange collaboration.[19]

No less interesting is the amount of animus directed at a man
who died over a hundred years ago. In the case of black militants,
hostility to Lincoln has no doubt been part of the process of
cutting loose from white America. Thus, there is little history but
much purpose in the statement of Malcolm X: "He probably did
more to trick Negroes than any other man in history."[20]

For white radicals too, rejection of Lincoln signified repudiation of the whole American cultural tradition, from the first
massacre of Indians to the Viet Nam War. In what might be called
the "malign consensus" school of United States history, Lincoln
remained the representative American, but the America that he
represented was a dark, ugly country, stained with injustice and
cruelty. Plainly, there is much more at stake here than the
reputation of a single historical figure.

James K. Vardaman, it is said, used to carry with him one
particular Lincoln quotation that he would whip out and read at
the slightest opportunity. This excerpt from the debate with
Douglas in 1858 at Charleston, Illinois, is now fast becoming the
most quoted passage in all of Lincoln's writings, outstripping even
the Gettysburg Address and the Second Inaugural. Pick up any
recent historical study of American race relations and somewhere
in its pages you are likely to find the following words.

I will say then that I am not, nor ever have been in favor of bringing about in
any way the social and political equality of the white and black races,—that I

[16] *Ibid.*, pp. 37-38, 40.
[17] Richard Claxton Gregory, *No More Lies: The Myth and the Reality of American History* (New York, 1971), p. 182.
[18] Bennett, "Lincoln a White Supremacist," p. 36.
[19] Davis, *Image*, p. 156: "There is something sadly ironic in seeing black extremists and Ku Kluxers clasping hands over the grave of the Great Emancipator's reputation."
[20] Robert Penn Warren, *Who Speaks for the Negro?* (New York, 1965), p. 262.

am not nor ever have been in favor of making voters or jurors of negroes, nor of qualifying them to hold office, nor to intermarry with white people; and I will say in addition to this that there is a physical difference between the white and black races which I believe will for ever forbid the two races living together on terms of social and political equality. And inasmuch as they cannot so live, while they do remain together there must be the position of superior and inferior, and I as much as any other man am in favor of having the superior position assigned to the white race.[21]

It is, of course, a quotation that bristles with relevancy. Problems that once preoccupied Lincoln's biographers, such as his part in bringing on the Civil War and the quality of his wartime leadership, have been more or less pushed aside by a question of newer fashion and greater urgency. It is well phrased in the preface to a collection of documents titled *Lincoln on Black and White* (1971): "Was Lincoln a racist? More important, how did Lincoln's racial views affect the course of our history?"[22]

Anyone who sets out conscientiously to answer such a query will soon find himself deep in complexity and confronting some of the fundamental problems of historical investigation. In one category are various questions about the historian's relation to the past: Is his task properly one of careful reconstruction, or are there more important purposes to be served? Does his responsibility include rendering moral judgments? If so, using what standards—those of his own time or those of the period under study? Then there are all the complications encountered in any effort to read the mind of a man, especially a politician, from the surviving record of his words and actions. For instance, what he openly affirmed as a youth may have been silently discarded in maturity; what he believed on a certain subject may be less significant than the intensity of his belief; and what he said on a certain occasion may have been largely determined by the immediate historical context, including the composition of his audience.

Terminological difficulties may also arise in the study of history, and such is the case with the word "racist," which serves us badly as a concept because of its denunciatory tone and indiscriminate use.[23] Conducive neither to objectivity nor to

[21] Roy P. Basler, ed., *The Collected Works of Abraham Lincoln* (9 vols.; New Brunswick, N.J., 1953-55), III, pp. 145-46.

[22] Arthur Zilversmit, ed., *Lincoln on Black and White* (Belmont, Calif., 1971),n.p.

[23] See Michael Banton, "The Concept of Racism," *in* Sami Zubaida, ed., *Race and Racialism* (London, 1970), pp. 17-34. The indiscriminate use of the word is well illustrated in the assertion of Robert Froman, *Racism* (New York, 1972), pp. 27-28, that

precision, the word has been employed so broadly that it is now being subdivided. Thus we are invited to distinguish between ideological racism and institutional racism,[24] between scientific racism and folk racism,[25] between active racism and inactive racism,[26] between racism and racial prejudice,[27] between racism and racialism,[28] and between hierachical racism and romantic racialism.[29] In its strictest sense, racism is a doctrine, but by extension it has also come to signify an attitude, a mode of behavior, and a social system. The *doctrine*, a work of intellectuals, is a rationalized theory of inherent Negro inferiority. In a given person, however, it can be anything from a casual belief to a philosophy of life. As an *attitude*, racism is virtually synonymous with prejudice—an habitual feeling of repugnance, and perhaps of enmity, toward members of another race. It can be anything from a mild tendency to a fierce obsession. Racism as a *mode of behavior* is prejudice activated in some way—a display of racial hostility that can be anything from mere avoidance of the other race to participation in a lynching. Racism as a *social system* means that law and custom combine to hold one race in subordination to another through institutional arrangements such as slavery, segregation, discrimination, and disfranchisement. Individuals can help support such a system with anything from tacit acquiescence to strenuous public service in its defense. These multiple and graduated meanings of the word "racism" are important to remember in exploring the historical convergence of Abraham Lincoln and the American Negro.[30]

---

there is a "racist overtone" to the statement that Columbus or Leif Ericson discovered America, because it implies that the Siberians who had arrived earlier "did not count."

[24] David M. Reimers, ed., *Racism in the United States: An American Dilemma?* (New York, 1972), p. 5.

[25] Banton, "Concept of Racism," p. 18.

[26] Forrest G. Wood, *Black Scare: The Racist Response to Emancipation and Reconstruction* (Berkeley, 1970), p. 15.

[27] George M. Fredrickson, *The Black Image in the White Mind: The Debate on Afro-American Character and Destiny, 1817-1914* (New York, 1971), p. 2.

[28] Margaret Nicholson, *A Dictionary of American-English Usage* (New York, 1958), p. 469.

[29] Fredrickson, *Black Image*, p. 101.

[30] *Webster's Third New International Dictionary* (Unabridged) defines "racism" as: "*1.* the assumption that psychocultural traits and capacities are determined by biological race and that races differ decisively from one another, which is usually coupled with a belief in the inherent superiority of a particular race and its right to domination over others. *2a.* a doctrine or political program based on the assumption of racism and designed to execute its principles. *2b.* a political or social system founded on racism. *3.* racialism."

"One must see him [Lincoln] first," says Bennett, "against the background of his times. Born into a poor white family in the slave state of Kentucky and raised in the anti-black environments of southern Indiana and Illinois, Lincoln was exposed from the very beginning to racism."[31] This is a familiar line of reasoning and credible enough on the surface. Any racial views encountered during his youth were likely to be unfavorable to the Negro. But more important is the question of how *often* he encountered such views and how *thoroughly* he absorbed them. Besides, the assumption that his racial attitudes were shaped more or less permanently by his early social environment does not take into account the fact that youth may rebel against established opinion. Lincoln did in a sense reject his father's world, leaving it behind him forever soon after reaching the age of twenty-one. Certainly his personal knowledge of black people was very limited. After catching a few glimpses of slavery as a small boy in Kentucky, he had little contact with Negroes while growing up in backwoods Indiana or as a young man in New Salem, Illinois. Those first twenty-eight years of his life take up just three pages in Benjamin Quarles' book, *Lincoln and the Negro.*[32]

If Lincoln entered manhood with strong feelings about race already implanted in his breast, one might expect to find indications of it in his earlier letters and speeches. For instance, on a steamboat carrying him home from a visit to Kentucky in 1841, there were a dozen slaves in chains. They had been, literally, sold down the river to a new master, and yet they seemed the most cheerful persons on board. Here was inspiration for some racist remarks in the "Sambo" vein, but Lincoln, describing the scene to a friend, chose instead to philosophize about the dubious effect of "condition upon human happiness." That is, he pictured Negroes behaving, as George M. Fredrickson puts it, "in a way that could be understood in terms of a common humanity and not as the result of peculiar racial characteristics."[33] Although one scholar may insist that Lincoln's racial beliefs were "matters of deep conviction,"[34] and another may talk about "the deep-rooted attitudes and ideas of a lifetime,"[35] there is scarcely any record of

[31] Bennett, "Lincoln a White Supremacist," p. 36.

[32] Benjamin Quarles, *Lincoln and the Negro* (New York, 1962), pp. 16-18.

[33] Fredrickson, "A Man but Not a Brother: Abraham Lincoln and Racial Equality," *Journal of Southern History* XLI (February 1975).

[34] George Sinkler, *The Racial Attitudes of American Presidents, from Abraham Lincoln to Theodore Roosevelt* (Garden City, N.Y., 1971), p. 75.

[35] Fredrickson, "A Man but Not a Brother."

his thoughts on race until he was past forty years of age. Long before then, of course, he had taken a stand against slavery, and it was the struggle over slavery that eventually compelled him to consider publicly the problem of race.

There is no escape from the dilemma that "relevance" makes the past worth studying and at the same time distorts it. We tend to see antebellum race and slavery in the wrong perspective. Race itself was not then the critical public issue that it has become for us. Only widespread emancipation could make it so, and, until the outbreak of the Civil War, that contingency seemed extremely remote. Our own preoccupation with race probably leads us to overestimate the importance of racial feeling in the antislavery movement.[36] In fact, there is a current disposition to assume that if a Republican did not have strong pro-Negro motives, he must have acted for strong anti-Negro reasons, such as a desire to keep the western territories lily-white.[37]

Actually, much of the motivation for antislavery agitation was only indirectly connected with the Negro. For example, the prime target often seemed to be not so much slavery as the "slave power," arrogant, belligerent, and overrepresented in all branches of the Federal government.[38] In Lincoln's case, no one can doubt his profound, though perhaps intermittent, sympathy for the slave. Yet he also hated slavery in a more abstract way as an evil principle and as a stain on the national honor, incompatible with the mission of America.[39]

It is a mistake to assume that Lincoln's actions in relation to the Negro were determined or even strongly influenced by his racial outlook. He based his antislavery philosophy, after all, squarely upon perception of the slave as a man, not as a Negro. According

---

[36] See Banton, "Concept of Racism," pp. 22-24, for the "inductivist explanation" of racism, which, he says, "is chiefly found in the writings of American sociologists. They are acquainted with racism in its modern forms and work backwards, viewing earlier statements about race from a modern standpoint instead of setting them in the intellectual context of the time in which they were made."

[37] For example, although he carefully qualifies his stated conclusions, this is the effect of Eugene H. Berwanger's *The Frontier Against Slavery: Western Anti-Negro Prejudice and the Slavery Extension Controversy* (Urbana, Ill., 1967).

[38] See Larry Gara, "Slavery and the Slave Power: A Crucial Distinction," *Civil War History* XV (1969), pp. 5-18.

[39] "Our republican robe is soiled, and trailed in the dust," said Lincoln in 1854. In the same speech, he called slavery a "monstrous injustice," and then added, "I hate it because it deprives our republican example of its just influence in the world." *Collected Works,* II, pp. 255, 276. Duberman, "Northern Response to Slavery," pp. 399-401, points to nationalism as one reason for opposition to abolitionism; but it should also be emphasized that national pride fortified the antislavery movement.

to the Declaration of Independence, he declared, all men, including black men, are created equal, at least to the extent that none has a right to enslave another. This became a point at issue in the famous debates with Stephen A. Douglas, who vehemently denied that the Declaration had anything to do with the African race. Lincoln, in turn, accused his rival of trying to "dehumanize" the Negro. But he had constructed an argument against slavery which, carried to its logical conclusion, seemed to spell complete racial equality. So Douglas insisted, anyhow, while Lincoln protested: "I do not understand that because I do not want a negro woman for a slave I must necessarily want her for a wife."[40]

Opponents of slavery everywhere had to contend with the charge that they advocated Negro equality. In the Democratic press, Republicans almost invariably became "Black Republicans," and political survival more often than not appeared to depend upon repudiation of the epithet. Thus the race question was most prominent in the antebellum period as a rhetorical and somewhat spurious feature of the slavery controversy.

Lincoln's first general remarks about racial equality on record were made in 1854, when the repeal of the Missouri Compromise drew him back to the center of Illinois politics. What to do, ideally, with southern slaves he pondered in a speech at Peoria. "Free them, and make them politically and socially our equals? My own feelings will not admit of this; and if mine would, we well know that those of the great mass of white people will not."[41] More often that year, however, he talked about the humanity of the Negro in denouncing the extension of slavery. Then came the election of 1856 and Fremont's defeat, which Lincoln analyzed with some bitterness: "We were constantly charged with seeking an amalgamation of the white and black races; and thousands turned from us, not believing the charge . . . but *fearing* to face it themselves."[42] It was at this point, significantly, that he became more aggressive and explicit in disavowing racial equality. He began using census figures to show that miscegenation was a by-product of slavery. He spoke of the "natural disgust" with which most white people viewed "the idea of indiscriminate amalgamation of the white and black races." And, under heavy pounding from Douglas during the senatorial campaign of 1858,

[40] *Collected Works* III, pp. 9-10, 29, 80, 95, 112-13, 146, 216, 280, 300-304, 470.

[41] *Ibid.*, II, pp. 255-256.

[42] *Ibid.*, II, p. 391.

he answered again and again in the manner of the notorious Charleston passage quoted above.[43] Indeed, his strongest feeling about race appears to have been his vexation with those who kept bringing the subject up. "Negro equality! Fudge!!" he scribbled on a piece of paper. "How long, in the government of a God great enough to make and maintain this Universe, shall there continue knaves to vend and fools to gulp, so low a piece of demagoguism as this?"[44]

Most of Lincoln's recorded generalizations about race were public statements made in the late 1850's as part of his running oratorical battle with Douglas.[45] Furthermore, nearly all of those statements were essentially disclaimers rather than affirmations. They indicated, for political reasons, the *maximum* that he was willing to deny the Negro and the *minimum* that he claimed for the Negro. They were concessions on points not at issue, designed to fortify him on the point that *was* at issue—namely, the extension of slavery. If he had responded differently at Charleston and elsewhere, the Lincoln of history simply would not exist. And words uttered in a context of such pressure may be less than reliable as indications of a man's lifetime attitude.

At least it seems possible that Lincoln's remarks in middle age on the subject of race were shaped more by his political realism than by impressions stamped on his mind in childhood. The principal intellectual influence, as Fredrickson has demonstrated, was Henry Clay, Lincoln's political hero, whom he studied anew for a eulogy delivered in 1852. Clay, in his attitude toward slavery, represented a link with the Founding Fathers. A slaveholder himself, who nevertheless believed that the institution was a "curse," he began and ended his career working for a program of gradual emancipation in Kentucky. He helped found and steadily supported the American Colonization Society. In his racial views, moreover, Clay emphasized the Negro's humanity and reserved judgment on the question of innate black inferiority. Lincoln not only adopted Clay's tentative, moderate outlook but extensively paraphrased and sometimes parroted his words.[46]

[43] *Ibid.*, II, pp. 405, 408; III, 16, 88, 249.

[44] *Ibid.*, III, p. 399.

[45] The principal exceptions are the Peoria speech of October 16, 1854, and the statement to the delegation of Negroes of August 14, 1862.

[46] Fredrickson, "A Man but Not a Brother." But for an argument belittling Clay's influence on Lincoln, see Marvin R. Cain, "Lincoln's Views on Slavery and the Negro: A Suggestion," *Historian*, XXVI (1964), pp. 502-20.

Considering, then, the peculiar context of his most significant remarks on the subject of race and considering also his dependence on Clay, it seems unwise to assert flatly, as some scholars do, that Lincoln embraced the doctrine of racism. Not that it would be astonishing to find that he did so. The assumption of inherent white superiority was almost universal and rested upon observation as well as prejudice. Comparison of European civilization and African "savagery" made it extremely difficult to believe in the natural equality of white and black races. Yet Lincoln's strongest statements, even if taken at face value and out of context, prove to be tentative and equivocal. He conceded that the Negro *might not* be his equal, or he said that the Negro *was not* his equal *in certain respects*. As an example, he named *color*, which certainly has a biological implication. But we cannot be certain that he was not merely expressing an aesthetic judgment or noting the social disadvantages of being black. He never used the word "inherent," or any of its equivalents, in discussing the alleged inferiority of the Negro, and it is not unlikely that he regarded such inferiority as resulting primarily from social oppression. In 1862, he compared blacks whose minds had been "clouded by slavery" with free Negroes "capable of thinking as white men." His last recorded disclaimer appears in a letter written as President-elect to a New York editor. He did not, it declared, "hold the black man to be the equal of the white, unqualifiedly." The final word throws away most of the declaration and scarcely suits a true ideological racist. Here there is a doubleness in the man as in the legend. It appears that he may have both absorbed and doubted, both shared and risen above, the racial doctrines of his time.[47]

Lincoln, who had four sons and no other children, was presumably never asked the ultimate racist question. He did indicate a disinclination to take a Negro woman for his wife, agreeing with most of his white contemporaries in their aversion to miscegenation. Otherwise, there is little evidence of racism as an attitude or racism as a mode of behavior in his relations with Negroes. Frederick Douglass, sometimes a severe critic of Lincoln's policies, said emphatically: "In all my interviews with Mr. Lincoln I was impressed with his entire freedom from popular prejudice against the colored race."[48] During the war years in Washington,

[47] *Collected Works*, III, p. 16; IV, p. 156; V, pp. 372-73.

[48] Allen Thorndike Rice, ed., *Reminiscences of Abraham Lincoln* (New York, 1888), p. 193.

the social status of Negroes underwent a minor revolution, exemplified in the arrival of a black diplomat from the newly recognized Republic of Haiti. Lincoln, according to Current, "opened the White House to colored visitors as no President had done before, and he received them in a spirit which no President has matched since."[49] Douglas and others appreciated not only his friendliness but his restraint. There was no effusiveness, no condescension. "He treated Negroes," says Quarles, "as they wanted to be treated—as human beings."[50]

On the other hand, Lincoln in the 1850's did plainly endorse the existing system of white supremacy, except for slavery. He defended it, however, on grounds of expediency rather than principle and on grounds of the incompatibility rather than the inequality of the races. Assuming that one race or the other must be on top, he admitted preferring that the superior position be *assigned* to the white race. Thus there was little association of institutional racism with ideological racism in his thinking.

Although Lincoln was by no means insensitive to the deprivation suffered by free Negroes,[51] he saw little hope of improving their condition and in any case regarded slavery as a far greater wrong. Moreover, it appeared that any serious attack on institutional racism would raise the cry of "Negro equality" and thereby damage the antislavery cause.

But then, if he hated slavery so much, why did Lincoln not become an abolitionist? There are several obvious reasons: fear for the safety of the Union, political prudence, constitutional scruples, a personal distaste for extremism, and perplexity over what to do with freed slaves.[52] In addition, it must be emphasized that Lincoln, as Lord Charnwood observed, "accepted the institutions to which he was born, and he enjoyed them."[53] Social reform was a fairly new phenomenon in antebellum America. Only a relatively small number of persons had adopted it as a life-style, and Lincoln cannot be counted among them. This author of the greatest reform in American history was simply not a reformer by nature.

[49] J. G. Randall and Richard N. Current, *Lincoln the President* (4 vols.; New York, 1945-55), IV, p. 316.

[50] Quarles, *Lincoln and the Negro*, p. 204.

[51] See especially his comment on an assertion by Roger B. Taney alleging that the Negro's status had improved since the framing of the Constitution, *Collected Works*, II, pp. 403-404.

[52] See discussion of factors discouraging abolitonism, *in* Duberman, "The Northern Response to Slavery," pp. 398-401.

[53] Lord Charnwood, *Abraham Lincoln* (New York, 1917), p. 455.

He even acquiesced in the retention of slavery, provided that it should not be allowed to expand. For him, the paramount importance of the Republican anti-extension program lay in its symbolic meaning as a commitment to the principle of ultimate extinction. Some later generation, he thought, would then convert the principle into practice. What this amounted to, in a sense, was antislavery tokenism, but it also proved to be a formula for the achievement of political power and, with it, the opportunity to issue a proclamation of emancipation.

Of course, it has been said that Lincoln deserves little credit for emancipation—that he came to it tardily and reluctantly under Radical duress. "Blacks have no reason to feel grateful to Abraham Lincoln," writes Julius Lester in *Look Out, Whitey! Black Power's Gon' Get Your Mama!* "How come it took him two whole years to free the slaves? His pen was sitting on his desk the whole time. All he had to do was get up one morning and say, 'Doggonnit! I think I'm gon' free the slaves today,' "[54] But *which* morning? That turned out to be the real question.

Lincoln, it should be remembered, was under strong pressure from *both* sides on the issue of emancipation, and so the Radical clamor alone will not explain his ultimate decision. Nevertheless, when the war began, many Americans quickly realized that the fate of slavery might be in the balance. Veteran abolitionists rejoiced that history was at last marching to their beat, and Lincoln did not fail to read what he called "the signs of the times." Emancipation itself, as he virtually acknowledged, came out of the logic of events, not his personal volition, but the time and manner of its coming were largely his choice.

There had been enough Republicans to win the presidential election, but there were not enough to win the war. They needed help from northern Democrats and border-state loyalists, who were willing to fight for the Union but not for abolition. A premature effort at emancipation might alienate enough support to make victory impossible. It would then be self-defeating, because there could be no emancipation without victory. Lincoln's remarkable achievement, whether he fully intended it or not, was to proclaim emancipation in such a way as to minimize disaffection. He did so by allowing enough time for the prospect to become domesticated in the public mind and by adhering scrupulously to the fiction

[54] Julius Lester, *Look Out, Whitey! Black Power's Gon' Get Your Mama!* (New York, 1968), p. 58.

that this momentous step was strictly a military measure. Much of the confusion about the Emancipation Proclamation results from taking too seriously Lincoln's verbal bowings and scrapings to the conservatives while all the time he was backing steadily away from them.[55]

The best illustration is his famous reply of August 22, 1862, to the harsh criticism of Horace Greeley, in which he said that his "paramount object" was to save the Union. "What I do about slavery, and the colored race," he declared, "I do because I believe it helps to save the Union; and what I forbear, I forbear because I do *not* believe it would help to save the Union."[56] The most striking thing about the entire document is its dissimulation. Although Lincoln gave the impression that options were still open, he had in fact already made up his mind, had committed himself to a number of persons, had drafted the Proclamation. Why, then, write such a letter? Because it was not a statement of policy but instead a brilliant piece of propaganda in which Lincoln, as Benjamin P. Thomas says, "used Greeley's outburst to prepare the people for what was coming."[57]

There were constitutional as well as political reasons, of course, for casting the Proclamation in military language and also for limiting its scope to those states and parts of states still in rebellion. In a sense, as historians fond of paradox are forever pointing out, it did not immediately liberate any slaves at all. And the Declaration of Independence, it might be added, did not immediately liberate a single colony from British rule. The people of Lincoln's time apparently had little doubt about the significance of the Proclamation. Jefferson Davis did not regard it as a mere scrap of paper, and neither did that most famous of ex-slaves, Frederick Douglass. He called it "the greatest event in our nation's history."[58]

In the long sweep of that history, emancipation had come on, not sluggishly, but with a rush and a roar—over a period of scarcely eighteen months. Given more time to reflect on its racial implications, white America might have recoiled from the act. Lincoln himself had never been anything but a pessimist about the

---

[55] For a good statement of Lincoln's strategy, see Hans L. Trefousse, *The Radical Republicans, Lincoln's Vanguard for Racial Justice* (New York, 1969), p. 182.

[56] *Collected Works*, V, pp. 388-89.

[57] Benjamin P. Thomas, *Abraham Lincoln* (New York, 1952), p. 342.

[58] Speech at Cooper Institute, February 1863, quoted in Zilversmit, *Lincoln on Black and White*, p. 133.

consequences of emancipation. Knowing full well the prejudices of his countrymen, he doubted that blacks and whites could ever live together amicably and on terms of equality. Over a century later, it is still too early to say that he was wrong.

With stark realism, Lincoln told a delegation of free Negroes in August 1862: "On this broad continent, not a single man of your race is made the equal of a single man of ours. Go where you are treated the best, and the ban is still upon you." And while blacks suffered from discrimination, whites suffered from the discord caused by the presence of blacks. "It is better for us both, therefore, to be separated," he said.[59] But Lincoln apparently never visualized a segregated America. For him, separation meant colonization, which, as a disciple of Henry Clay, he had been advocating at least since 1852. Perhaps the strangest feature of Lincoln's presidential career was the zeal with which he tried to promote voluntary emigration of free Negroes to Africa or Latin America. He recommended it in his first two annual messages, urged it upon Washington's black leadership, and endorsed it in his preliminary Emancipation Proclamation. He had foreign capitals circulated in a search for likely places of settlement. Furthermore, with funds supplied by Congress, he launched colonization enterprises in Haiti and Panama, both of which proved abortive.[60]

What surprises one the most about these almost frantic activities is their petty scale. Lincoln implored the delegation of Washington Negroes to find him a hundred, or fifty, or even twenty-five families willing to emigrate. The Haitian project, if completely successful, would have accommodated just five thousand persons—about the number of Negroes born every two weeks in the United States. It would have required an enormous effort even to hold the black population stable at four and one-half million, let alone reduce it appreciably. Back in 1854, Lincoln had admitted the impracticability of colonization as anything but a long-range program.[61] Why, then, did he betray such feverish haste to make a token beginning in 1862?

One interesting answer emerges from the chronology. Most of the colonization flurry took place during the second half of 1862. After that, Lincoln's interest waned, although, according to the dubious testimony of Benjamin F. Butler, it revived near the end

[59] *Collected Works*, V, p. 372.
[60] Quarles, *Lincoln and the Negro*, pp. 108-23, 191-94.
[61] *Collected Works*, II, p. 255.

of the war.[62] After issuing the Emancipation Proclamation on January 1, 1863, Lincoln never made another public appeal for colonization. It appears that his spirited activity in the preceding six months may have been part of the process of conditioning the public mind for the day of jubilee. The promise of colonization had always been in part a means of quieting fears about the racial consequences of manumission. Offered as the ultimate solution to the problem of the black population, it could also serve as a psychological safety valve for the problem of white racism. This combination of purposes had inspired a number of Republican leaders to take up the cause of colonization in the late 1850's. One of them, the brother of his future postmaster-general, had told Lincoln then that the movement would "ward off the attacks made upon us about Negro equality."[63]

In his second annual message of December 1, 1862, Lincoln said, "I cannot make it better known than it already is, that I strongly favor colonization." Then he continued in a passage that has received far less attention: "And yet I wish to say there is an objection urged against free colored persons remaining in the country, which is largely imaginary, if not sometimes malicious." He went on to discuss and minimize the fear that freedmen would displace white laborers, after which he wrote:

But it is dreaded that the freed people will swarm forth, and cover the whole land? Are they not already in the land? Will liberation make them any more numerous? Equally distributed among the whites of the whole country, and there would be but one colored to seven whites. Could the one, in any way, greatly disturb the seven? There are many communities now, having more than one free colored person, to seven whites; and this, without any apparent consciousness of evil from it.[64]

Here, along with his last public endorsement of colonization, was an eloquent plea for racial accommodation at home. The one might remain his ideal ultimate solution, but the other, he knew, offered the only hope in the immediate future.

Yet, if his plans for Reconstruction are an accurate indication,

[62] Benjamin F. Butler, *Butler's Book* (Boston, 1892), pp. 903-8.

[63] Eric Foner, *Free Soil, Free Labor, Free Men: The Ideology of the Republican Party before the Civil War* (New York, 1970), p. 271. See also, Harry V. Jaffa, *Crisis of the House Divided: An Interpretation of the Issues in the Lincoln-Douglas Debates* (Garden City, N.Y., 1959), p. 61.

[64] *Collected Works*, V, pp. 534-35. See also Lincoln's letter to John A. Andrew, February 18, 1864, *in* VII, p. 191.

Lincoln at the time of his death had given too little consideration to the problem of racial adjustment and to the needs of four million freedmen. How much that would have changed if he had not been killed has been the subject of lively controversy.[65] Certainly his policies by 1865 no longer reflected all the views expressed in 1858, when he had repudiated both Negro citizenship and Negro suffrage. Now, by fiat of his administration in defiance of the Dred Scott decision, blacks were citizens of the United States, and he had begun in a gentle way to press for limited black enfranchisement. He had overcome his initial doubts about enlisting Negroes as fighting soldiers, was impressed by their overall performance, and thought they had earned the right to vote.

Lincoln once told Charles Sumner that on the issue of emancipation they were only four to six weeks apart.[66] The relative earliness of his first favorable remarks about Negro enfranchisement suggests that he had again read the "signs of the times." It is not difficult to believe that after the war he would have continued closer to the Sumners than to the conservatives whom he had placated but never followed for long. And one can scarcely doubt that his postwar administration would have been more responsive to Negro aspirations than Andrew Johnson's proved to be.

But for several reasons Lincoln's role was likely to be more subdued than we might expect from the Great Emancipator. First, during peacetime, with his powers and responsibilities as Commander-in-Chief greatly reduced, he probably would have yielded more leadership to Congress in the old Whig tradition. Second, at the time of his death, he still regarded race relations as primarily a local matter, just as he had maintained during the debates with Douglas: "I do not understand there is any place where an alteration of the social and political relations of the Negro and white man can be made except in the State Legislature."[67] Third, Negroes as Negroes were nearly always connotative in Lincoln's thinking. Their welfare, though by no means a matter of indiffer-

---

[65] See especially William B. Hesseltine, *Lincoln's Plan of Reconstruction* (Tuscaloosa, Ala., 1960); Ludwell H. Johnson, "Lincoln and Equal Rights: The Authenticity of the Wadsworth Letter," *Journal of Southern History* XXXII (1966), pp. 83-87; Harold Hyman, "Lincoln and Equal Rights for Negroes: The Irrelevancy of the 'Wadsworth Letter,' " *Civil War History* XII (1966), pp. 258-66; Ludwell H. Johnson, "Lincoln and Equal Rights: A Reply," *Civil War History* XIII (1967), pp. 66-73.

[66] Trefousse, *Radical Republicans*, pp. 210-11.

[67] *Collected Works*, III, p. 146.

ence to him, had never been, and was not likely to become, his "paramount object." They were, in the words of Frederick Douglass, "only his stepchildren."[68]   Finally, in his attitude toward the wrongs of the free Negro, Lincoln had none of the moral conviction that inspired his opposition to slavery. He never seems to have suspected that systematic racial discrimination might be, like slavery, a stain on the national honor and a crime against mankind. Whether that is the measure of his greatness must be left to each one's personal taste. Of Copernicus we might say: What a genius! He revolutionized our understanding of the solar system. Or: What an ignoramus! He did not understand the rest of the universe at all.

[68] *Life and Times of Frederick Douglass, Written by Himself* (New York, 1962 reprint of 1892 edition), p. 485.

GEORGE M. FREDRICKSON

Blue Over Gray:
Sources of Success and Failure
in the Civil War

HISTORIANS HAVE EXPENDED vast amounts of time, energy, and ingenuity searching for the causes and consequences of the Civil War. Much less effort has been devoted to explaining the outcome of the war itself. Yet the question is obviously important. One only has to imagine how radically different the future of North America would have been had the South won its permanent independence. It is also possible that a full comparison of how the two sides responded to the ultimate test of war will shed reflex light on both the background and legacy of the conflict. If northern success and southern failure can be traced to significant differences in the two societies as they existed on the eve of the war, then we may have further reason for locating the origins of the war in the clash of divergent social systems and ideologies. If the relative strengths of the North in wartime were rooted in the character of its society, then the sources of northern victory would foreshadow, to some extent at least, the postwar development of a nation reunited under northern hegemony.

.A number of plausible explanations of "why the North won"

have been advanced.[1] The problem with most of them is not that they are wrong but that they are partial or incomplete. What is needed is not the unearthing of new "factors" propelling the South down the road to Appomattox but a broader frame of reference allowing for a synthesis of these familiar explanations into a more comprehensive interpretation.

Perhaps the most widely accepted explanation of why the North won and the South lost derives from the time-honored proposition that God is on the side of the heaviest battalions.[2] The North's advantages in manpower, resources, and industrial capacity were clearly overwhelming. According to the census of 1860, the Union, not counting the contested border states of Missouri and Kentucky, had a population of approximately 20,275,000. The Confederacy, on the other hand, had a white population of only about 5,500,000. If we include the 3,654,000 blacks, the total population of the eleven Confederate states adds up to slightly more than 9,000,000. Even if we consider the black population an asset to the Confederacy in carrying on a war for the preservation of slavery, the North still ends up with a more than two-to-one advantage in population. There was an even greater differential in readily available manpower of military age; the northern advantage in this respect was well in excess of three-to-one. In industrial capacity, the Union had an enormous edge. In 1860, the North had approximately 110,000 manufacturing establishments manned by about 1,300,000 workers, while the South had only 18,000 establishments with 110,000 workers. Thus for every southern industrial worker the North had a factory or workshop! Finally, in railroad mileage, so crucial to the logistics of the Civil War, the North possessed over seventy percent of the nation's total of 31,256 miles.[3]

With such a decisive edge in manpower, industrial plant, and transportation facilities, how, it might well be asked, could the North possibly have lost? Yet history shows many examples of the physically weaker side winning, especially in wars of national

[1] See especially the essays by Richard N. Current, T. Harry Williams, Norman A. Graebner, David Donald, and David M. Potter in David Donald, ed., *Why the North Won The Civil War* (New York, 1962); Kenneth M. Stampp, *The Southern Road to Appomattox* Cotton Memorial Papers, 4 (El Paso, Tex., 1969); and Bell I. Wiley, *The Road to Appomattox* (New York, 1968).

[2] See Richard N. Current, "God and the Strongest Battalions," in Donald, ed., *Why the North Won*, pp. 15-32.

[3] Allan Nevins, *The War for the Union: The Improvised War, 1861-1862* (New York, 1959), pp. 424-26 (Vol. 1 of *The War for the Union*).

independence. The achievement of Dutch independence from Spain in the seventeenth century, the colonists' success in the American Revolution, and many "wars of national liberation" in the twentieth century, including the Algerian revolution and the long struggle for Vietnamese self-determination, provide examples of how the physically weaker side can prevail. In popularly supported wars for national independence, the "imperial" power faces a much more difficult task than the separatist rebels. The former must conquer and hold the territory of a hostile population; the latter need only defend themselves and inflict enough damage on the invaders to convince them that ultimate victory in a long and costly struggle is not worth the sacrifice. Southern secessionists believed they could win—and historical precedent seemed to be on their side—partly because they could not conceive of the North making the sustained effort required to bring its full strength to bear in the struggle. By itself, the physical differential will not explain why the North emerged victorious. What we really need to know is how it was possible for the North to mobilize and utilize its advantages with sufficient effect to deny the South's bid for independence.

Recognizing the insufficiency of a crude economic or demographic explanation, some historians have sought psychological reasons for the Confederate defeat. It has been argued that the South "whipped itself" because it did not believe strongly enough in its cause. While the North could allegedly call on the full fervor of American nationalism and antislavery idealism, the South was saddled with the morally dubious enterprise of defending slavery and was engaged in breaking up a union of hallowed origin for which many southerners still had a lingering reverence. It has even been suggested that large numbers of loyal Confederates had a subconscious desire to lose the war. The northern victory is therefore ascribed to the fact that the North had a better cause and thus higher morale; the breakdown in the South's will to win is seen as the consequence of a deep ambivalence about the validity of the whole Confederate enterprise.[4]

This thesis is highly speculative and not easily reconciled with the overall pattern of pro-Confederate sentiment and activity. It would seem to underestimate or even to belittle the willingness of large numbers of southerners to fight and die for the Confederacy.

[4] See Stampp, *The Southern Road to Appomattox, passim*; Roy F. Nichols, *Blueprints for Leviathan: American Style* (New York, 1963), pp. 238-239; and Wiley, *Road to Appomattox*, pp. 102-5.

No northerner who fought the "Rebs" at places such as Shiloh, Antietam, and Gettysburg would have concluded that the South really wanted to lose. It seems unlikely that the massive suffering of the southern population, both on the battlefield and the homefront, could have been endured for as long as it was if a substantial majority had not really believed in what they were fighting for. To imply that the southern cause could not possibly have aroused genuine enthusiasm because it was incompatible with modern liberal principles seems both present-minded and condescending. A commitment to slavery as a source of prosperity and a secure basis for racial hegemony was undoubtedly at the root of southern nationalism. But nationalism *in extremis* has a way of transcending its origins. Even southerners who had strong misgivings about slavery—and they were probably a minority— could readily and plausibly define their cause as a defense of local liberty against coercion by an alien government. As the example of Robert E. Lee clearly demonstrates, a man of this type could even become the embodiment of the Confederate cause. Once columns of Yankee soldiers began to darken the southern landscape, doubts and misgivings were inevitably lost in a surge of aggrieved patriotism: The homeland was being invaded by representatives of a government and a society that southerners, their attitudes shaped by a generation of sectional controversy and propaganda, had come to regard as irreconcilably alien and hostile.

On the surface at least, it seems harder to explain what made the northern cause so compelling. Contrary to antislavery mythology, there is little evidence to sustain the view that a genuinely humanitarian opposition to black servitude ever animated a majority of the northern population. Most northerners defined their cause as the preservation of the Union, not the emancipation of the slaves. This was made explicit in a joint resolution of Congress, passed overwhelmingly in July 1861, denying any federal intention to interfere with the domestic institutions of the southern states. When emancipation came, it was presented and justified as a necessary war measure rather than as an ideological imperative. Even so, there was an unfavorable reaction in many parts of the North. Partly as a result of widespread opposition to the preliminary Emancipation Proclamation of September 20, 1862, the Republicans suffered heavy losses in the subsequent fall elections. Unlike the abolitionist call for an antislavery crusade, the cause of the Union could and did arouse the majority to strenuous endeavor. But when considered simply as a formal ideology,

Unionism seems too abstract and remote from the concrete interests of ordinary people to have sustained, simply through its own intrinsic motivating force, the enthusiasm necessary for such a long and bloody conflict. In any case, the *a priori* proposition that the North had a more compelling cause, and therefore one that was bound to generate higher morale, seems questionable.

Morale in both sections fluctuated in direct response to the fortunes of war. In the fall and winter of 1862-1863, morale was high in the South and low in the North, principally because at that point the South was winning most of the battles. After the Union victories at Gettysburg and Vicksburg in July 1863, the situation was understandably reversed. In May and June of 1864, southern morale made a temporary and limited recovery when Grant was repulsed in Virginia and Sherman checked in Georgia. As might be expected, northern enthusiasm waned at the same time and only revived when Sherman captured Atlanta in September and began his march to the sea. Throughout the conflict, morale seems to have been more a function of military victory and success than a cause of it. Furthermore, any comparison involving the will to win of the respective sides cannot ignore the different situations that they faced. Except for Lee's brief forays into Maryland and Pennsylvania, the northern people never had to suffer from invasion of their own territory. Whether the North's allegedly superior morale and determination would have stood up under pressures equivalent to those experienced by the South will never be known. But we do know that the resolve of the North came dangerously close to breaking in the summer of 1864, at a time when its territory was secure, its economy booming, and its ultimate victory all but assured. At exactly the same time, the South was girding for another nine months of desperate struggle despite economic collapse and the loss of much of its territory. Such a comparison hardly supports the thesis that the North excelled the South in its will to win. What we still need to know is how the North remained strong enough politically, militarily, and economically to gain the practical successes necessary to prevent its precarious morale situation from getting out of hand and why the South on the other hand suffered a kind of institutional collapse which meant that it could not hope to win no matter how much effort and dedication it expended.

Some have attributed the North's success in outlasting the South to its superior leadership. One distinguished historian has even suggested that if the North and South had exchanged

Presidents the outcome of the war would have been reversed.[5] As a wartime President, Lincoln was unquestionably superior to Davis. A master politician, Lincoln was able through a combination of tact and forcefulness to hold together the bitterly antagonistic factions of the Republican party. Within his own cabinet, the full spectrum of Republican opinion was represented, and Lincoln's masterful handling of the rivalry between Secretary of State Seward and Secretary of the Treasury Chase was indicative of his success in containing a potentially disruptive struggle between the conservative and the radical wings of his party. Lincoln was also able to reach out to a portion of the Democratic party; in the election of 1864, he successfully ran at the head of a Union coalition with a war Democrat as his vice presidential candidate. Lincoln was similarly skillful in his relations with the war governors. At the outset of the conflict, the Republican governors dominated the party and took the lead in organizing the North for war. Gradually but firmly Lincoln assumed direction of the governors' activities and without losing their support succeeded in stripping them of much of their independent military and political authority. He taught them to work in harness with a strong national administration and to subordinate local interests and local pride to the larger needs of the Union cause.[6] But perhaps Lincoln's greatest successes came in his role as commander in chief of the armed forces. Although lacking military training and experience, he had a good instinctive grasp of broad strategic considerations. Furthermore, he knew that he had neither the time nor the tactical ability to take direct charge of military operations and wisely refrained from interfering directly with his generals except when their excessive caution or incompetence gave him no choice. Lincoln's primary objective was to find a general who had a comprehensive view of strategic needs, a willingness to fight, and consequently the ability to take full charge of military activity. In late 1863, he found the right man and without hesitation turned the entire military effort over to General Grant, who proceeded to fight the war to a successful conclusion. In innumerable ways, Lincoln gave evidence of his common sense, flexibility, and willingness to learn from experience. Although not the popular demigod he would become after his assassination, he did provide

[5] David M. Potter, "Jefferson Davis and the Political Factors in Confederate Defeat," in Donald, ed., *Why the North Won*, pp. 109-10.

[6] See William B. Hesseltine, *Lincoln and the War Governors* (New York, 1949).

inspiration to the North as a whole. Many who had been critical of Lincoln at the start of the war, seeing him merely as a rough, inexperienced, frontier politician, came to recognize the quality of his statesmanship. Furthermore, his eloquence at Gettysburg and in the Second Inaugural helped to give meaning and resonance to the northern cause.

The leadership of Davis was of a very different caliber. The Confederate President was a proud, remote, and quarrelsome man with a fatal passion for always being in the right and for standing by his friends, no matter how incompetent or unpopular they turned out to be. He fought constantly with his cabinet and sometimes replaced good men who had offended him with second-raters who would not question his decisions. His extraordinary tactlessness and his unwillingness to compromise or accommodate himself to the opinions or personalities of others made it inevitable that he would become involved in serious feuds with most of the influential men of the Confederacy. He acquired bitter enemies in Congress, among the Confederate governors, and among the most competent southern generals. Most southern newspapers were virulently anti-Davis by the end of the war. Particularly harmful was Davis' military role. Because he had commanded forces in the Mexican war and served as Secretary of War of the United States, he thought of himself as qualified to direct all phases of operations. This belief in his own military genius, combined with a constitutional inability to delegate authority, led to excessive interference with his generals and to some very questionable strategic decisions, particularly those stemming from his adherence to a rigid policy of troop dispersal and departmentalization of command. Davis seemed to believe that the heavens would fall if the bureaucratic rules of a peacetime army were violated. Refusing to follow Lincoln's example and delegate overall authority to a general in chief, he had all departments report directly to him—an arrangement that made effective coordination of the South's limited military forces all but impossible. Finally, he played favorites among his generals, basing preferences more on personal likes and dislikes than on military performance. Offended by the independence of Beauregard and Joseph E. Johnston, he deprived these generals of important commands and failed to make full use of their talents. On the other hand, he stuck by his friend, the incompetent General Bragg, after almost everyone else in the Confederacy had lost faith in him. Even Robert E. Lee, the most tactful of men and a general with a very narrow conception of his proper sphere of action, had problems with Davis. Davis' great preoccupation with military affairs, while disastrous in itself, also meant that he had little time for his other responsibilities. Unlike Lincoln, he lost touch with the political situation, and he failed to provide leadership in the critical area of economic policy. In the end, one has a picture of Davis tinkering ineffectually with the South's military machine while a whole society was crumbling around him.

It appears the North had a great war leader, and the South a weak one. Can we therefore explain the outcome of the Civil War as an historical accident, a matter of northern luck in finding someone who could do the job and southern misfortune in picking the wrong man? Before we come to this beguilingly simple conclusion, we need to take a broader look at northern and southern leadership and raise the question of whether the kind of leadership a society produces is purely accidental. If Lincoln was a great leader of men, it was at least partly because he had good material to work with. Seward was in some ways a brilliant Secretary of State; Stanton directed the War Department with great determination and efficiency; and even Chase, despite his awkward political maneuvering, was on the whole a competent Secretary of the Treasury. On Capitol Hill, a new leadership emerged that by 1863 had drafted and passed a greater mass of legislation than any previous Congress, legislation that not only contributed to the North's ability to wage war but also helped lay the groundwork for the postwar economic development of the nation.[7] Some of the war governors, men like John Andrew of Massachusetts and Eli Morton of Indiana, were extraordinarily energetic and capable administrators. One area where the North lacked effective leaders for the first two and a half years of the war was on the battlefield; but with the emergence of Grant and Sherman this void was more than filled. The North, it can be argued, had not simply one great leader but was able during the war to develop competent and efficient leadership on almost all levels. Such a pattern could hardly have been accidental; more likely it reveals something about the capacity of northern society to produce men of talent and initiative who could deal with the unprecedented problems of a total war.

In the Confederacy, the situation was quite different. Among

[7]See Leonard P. Curry, *Blueprint for Modern America: Nonmilitary Legislation of the First Civil War Congress* (Nashville, Tenn., 1968).

the South's generals there of course were some brilliant tactical commanders. Their successes on the battlefield were instrumental in keeping the Confederacy afloat for four years. But, in almost all other areas, the South revealed a sad lack of capable leadership. In fairness to Davis, it has to be recognized that many of the politicians with whom he quarreled were more than his match when it came to testiness and inflexibility. Senator Louis T. Wigfall of Texas, one of the administration's archenemies, seems to have been no more than a coarse and colorful replica of the President he constantly denounced. Much of the criticism of Davis was not directed at his real shortcomings but was either petty or blatantly unfair. A good deal of it was based on the absurd charge that Davis was trying to make himself a dictator. Confederate Congressmen fought constantly with each other, sometimes violently, and produced a meager legislative record. In their last session before Appomattox, they attended to routine matters in a desultory way, manifesting little awareness of the impending northern victory. The behavior of some southern governors can only be described as scandalous. Instead of working for the common cause as their northern counterparts did, they spent their time defending "states' rights" and local interests against the urgent efforts of the Confederate government to mobilize men and resources. Governors Joe E. Brown of Georgia and Rupert Vance of North Carolina demonstrated a positive genius for the obstruction of Confederate policies. Leadership failure in the South, therefore, cannot be blamed exclusively or even principally on Jefferson Davis. It reflected the strange inability of a whole society to produce leaders who could cooperate effectively in the defense of a cause in which they all professed to believe. It is an extraordinary fact that among the men who did most to undermine Confederate unity were some of the most fervent southern nationalists.

The contrast in leadership, therefore, would seem to reflect some deeper differences of a kind that would make one section more responsive than the other to the practical demands of fighting a large-scale war. Since both societies faced unprecedented challenges, success would depend to a great extent on which side had the greater ability to adjust to new situations. Key elements in such an adjustment would be the readiness to innovate and the capacity to organize. Lincoln summed up a characteristic northern attitude in his Annual Message to Congress on December 1, 1862: "The dogmas of the quiet past, are inadequate to the stormy

present. The occasion is piled high with difficulty, and we must
rise with the occasion. As our case is new, we must think anew. We
must disenthrall ourselves, and then we shall save our country."[8]

Lincoln himself set the pattern for precedent-breaking innovation. Whenever he felt obligated to assume extra-constitutional powers to deal with situations unforeseen by the Constitution, he did so with little hesitation. After the outbreak of the
war and before Congress was in session to sanction his actions, he
expanded the regular army, advanced public money to private
individuals, and declared martial law on a line from Washington to
Philadelphia. On September 24, 1862, again without Congressional
authorization, he extended the jurisdiction of martial law and
suspended the writ of habeas corpus in all cases of alleged
disloyalty. The Emancipation Proclamation can also be seen as an
example of extra-constitutional innovation. Acting under the
amorphous concept of "the war powers" of the President, Lincoln
struck at slavery primarily because "military necessity" dictated
new measures to disrupt the economic and social system of the
enemy. There was bitter opposition in some quarters to such
unprecedented assertions of executive power, but a majority in
Congress and in the country accepted the argument of necessity
and supported the President's actions.

The spirit of innovation was manifested in other areas as well.
In Grant and Sherman the North finally found generals who
grasped the nature of modern war and were ready to jettison
outworn rules of strategy and tactics. "If men make war in slavish
observance of rules, they will fail . . . ," said Grant in summing up
his military philosophy. "War is progressive, because all the
instruments and elements of war are progressive."[9] In his march
from Atlanta to the sea in the fall of 1864, Sherman introduced
for the first time the modern strategy of striking directly at the
enemy's domestic economy. The coordinated, multipronged offensive launched by Grant in 1864, of which Sherman's march was
a critical component, was probably the biggest, boldest, and most
complex military operation mounted anywhere before the twentieth century. Grant, like Lincoln, can be seen as embodying the
North's capacity for organization and innovation.

The necessity of supplying and servicing the massive Union

[8] Roy P. Basler, ed., *The Collected Works of Abraham Lincoln* (New Brunswick,
N.J., 1953), V, p. 536.

[9] As quoted in T. Harry Williams, "The Military Leadership of North and South," in
Donald, ed., *Why the North Won*, pp. 51-52; see also J. F. C. Fuller, *Grant and Lee: A
Study in Personality and Generalship* (Bloomington, Ind., 1957), p. 82.

army also led to some startling departures from traditional practices. When necessary, railroads were seized and operated by the government. (Some were even built by the government.) Federal administration of the railroads not only facilitated the movement of men and materials but also helped unify the nation's system by connecting separated lines and standardizing gauges. The need to care for hordes of wounded men led to a number of innovations and improvements in medical services. The building and operation of great military hospitals both encouraged the rapid development of new therapeutic methods and helped revolutionize hospital administration. Major advances in the science of sanitation as well as aid in the distribution of medical supplies took place under the auspices of the United States Sanitary Commission, an extraordinary instrument of private philanthropy operating on a national scale.

Businessmen also responded to the crisis and found that what was patriotic could also be highly profitable. There were the inevitable frauds perpetrated on the government by contractors, but more significant was the overall success of the industrial system in producing the goods required. Since manufacturers in many lines now had a guaranteed national market, they had every incentive to expand operations and increase efficiency. A new kind of large-scale industrial enterprise began to come into existence as entrepreneurial energies responded vigorously to new opportunities. Military demand encouraged expansion and consolidation in such industries as iron and steel, ready-to-wear clothing, shoes, meat packing, and even pocket watches. The reaper industry underwent a huge expansion, as farmers, adjusting to a wartime labor shortage, mechanized their operations and actually increased production of grains to such an extent that they not only met the domestic need but exported enough to make up for the slack in American exports caused by the blockade of southern cotton. On the whole, the northern economy adapted so successfully to war that the nation enjoyed increasing prosperity on the home front in the very midst of civil war. No small part of this success was due to the willingness of businessmen, farmers, and government procurement officials to "think and act anew" by organizing themselves into larger and more efficient units for the production, transportation, and allocation of goods.[10]

---

[10] On how the North organized for war on the home front see Allan Nevins, *The War for the Union: The War Becomes Revolution, 1862-1863* (New York, 1960), pp. 456-511 (Vol. II of *The War for the Union*).

It would be an understatement to say that the South demonstrated less capacity than the North for organization and innovation. In fact, the South's most glaring failures were precisely in the
area of coordination and collective adaptation to new conditions.
The Confederacy did of course manage to put an army in the field
that was able to hold the North at bay for four years. And it kept
that army reasonably well supplied with arms, due mainly to the
prodigious efforts of Josiah Gorgas, chief of the Confederate
Bureau of Ordnance. Gorgas, a Pennsylvanian by birth, was
probably the South's boldest and most effective organizer and
innovator. From nothing, he personally built up a modern mu-
nitions industry sufficient to meet the needs of the Confederate
army.[11] But Gorgas was quite exceptional; there were few others
like him in the Confederacy. Southern successes on the battlefield
were in no real sense triumphs of organization or innovation.
Before the rise of Grant and Sherman, most Civil War battles were
fought according to the outdated tactical principles that generals
on both sides had learned at West Point. In these very conventional battles, the South had the advantage because it had the
most intelligent and experienced of the West Pointers. Since
everyone played by the same rules, it was inevitable that those
who could play the game best would win. When the rules were
changed by Grant and Sherman, the essential conservatism and
rigidity of southern military leadership became apparent.

Besides being conventional in their tactics, southern armies were
notoriously undisciplined; insubordination was an everyday occurrence and desertion eventually became a crippling problem. There
were so many men absent without leave by August 1, 1863, that a
general amnesty for deserters had to be declared. For full effectiveness, southern soldiers had to be commanded by generals such
as Robert E. Lee and Stonewall Jackson, charismatic leaders who
could command the personal loyalty and respect of their men. The
idea of obeying an officer simply because of his rank went against
the southern grain.[12]

Although the army suffered from the excessive individualism of
its men and the narrow traditionalism of its officers, these defects

[11] On Gorgas' achievements see Allan Nevins, *The War for the Union: The Organized
War, 1863-1864* (New York, 1971), pp. 16-19 (Vol. III of *The War for the Union*).

[12] For an interpretation of the Confederate army's disciplinary problems, see David
Donald, "Died of Democracy," in Donald, ed., *Why the North Won*, pp. 79-84, and
another essay by Donald, "The Southerner as a Fighting Man," in Charles Grier Sellers,
Jr., ed., *The Southerner as American*, (Chapel Hill, N.C., 1960), pp. 72-88.

were not fatal until very late in the war, mainly because it took the North such a long time to apply its characteristic talent for organization and innovation directly to military operations. But on the southern home front similar attitudes had disastrous consequences almost from the beginning. In its efforts to mobilize the men and resources of the South, the Confederate government was constantly hamstrung by particularistic resistance to central direction and by a general reluctance to give up traditional ideas and practices incompatible with the necessities of war.

Particularism was manifested most obviously in the refusal of state governments to respond to the needs of the Confederacy. The central government was rudely rebuffed when it sought in 1861 to get the states to give up control over the large quantity of arms in their possession. The states held back for their own defense most of the 350,000 small arms that they held. The Confederacy, initially able to muster only 190,000 weapons, was forced to turn down 200,000 volunteers in the first year of the war because it could not arm them. The states also held back men. In 1862, when McClellan was threatening Richmond, the approximately 100,000 men held in state service were unavailable for defending the Confederate capital or for any other significant military operations. When manpower problems forced the adoption of conscription in 1862, some southern governors worked openly and successfully to obstruct it. Governor Brown of Georgia came close to resorting to the old southern tactic of nullification in his efforts to prevent Georgians from being drafted to fight for the Confederacy. After his stance of outright defiance was declared unconstitutional by the state Supreme Court, Brown resorted to more devious tactics. Noting that the Confederate conscription law exempted public officials and militia officers, Brown proceeded to appoint men of draft age in large numbers to nominal public offices and made wholesale promotions from enlisted to officer rank in the militia. In 1864 when Sherman was besieging Atlanta, Brown still refused to place his 10,000-man state army under Confederate command and thus withheld it from the defense of his own capital. State governments also hindered Confederate efforts to provide the army with adequate supplies of food and clothing. Some states insisted on provisioning only their own troops. North Carolina, the center of the southern cotton industry, reserved the production of its mills almost exclusively for North Carolina regiments. In the last days of the war when Lee's army was fighting in rags, North Carolina was still holding in its warehouses 92,000 uniforms, along with thousands of blankets, tents, and shoes.[13]

It would be misleading, however, to attach too much importance to the states' rights philosophy *per se* as a source of difficulties of this kind. In much the same way that states' rights had been used as a facade for the social and economic interests of slaveholders before the war, it was utilized during the war by local interests that wished to avoid effective regulation. These interests found it easier to manipulate state governments than to deal with Richmond. A case in point is the history of attempts to regulate the shippers engaged in running the Union blockade. Blockade runners made their greatest profits when they imported luxury goods for the open market and exported privately owned cotton. The vital interests of the Confederacy demanded, on the other hand, that priority be given to the importation of war materials and the export of cotton the government had acquired through loans and taxation "in kind." The blockade runners, with the connivance of state governments, had great success in foiling Confederate efforts to control their cargoes. In 1863, shipowners were finally pressured into an agreement to rent one third of the space on every vessel to the Confederate government. But they quickly nullified this arrangement by allowing themselves to be chartered by the states, a device that effectively froze out Confederate goods. In 1864, Richmond made another attempt to gain control of shipping, this time passing a law that enabled President Davis to reserve one half the cargo space on all outgoing and incoming ships. The result was a strike of the blockade runners lasting several weeks which did serious damage to an already crumbling economy. The state governments condoned and even supported the strike because they regarded the shippers as local interests to be regulated, if at all, by the states rather than the central government. In this instance, states' rights and laissez-faire economic attitudes combined to favor private interests over public needs.[14]

The South's strong commitment to economic laissez-faire hindered the Confederate cause even more dramatically in railroad policy. Although the Confederacy had a more pressing need than the North to make effective use of its limited rail facilities, it was

---

[13] Frank Owsley, *State Rights in the Confederacy* (Chicago, 1925), pp. 63-73, 119-20, 126-27, 203-8, 272-3, and *passim*.

[14] *Ibid.*, pp. 124-49.

slower to assert direct control over the system. For most of the war, the government tried ineffectually to control the railroads through a series of voluntary agreements. Not until February 1865 was it given the right to seize and operate the lines. Thus shipping and railroads, the external and internal lifelines of the Confederacy, resisted effective control and coordination until the war was already lost—striking examples of how economic particularism impeded the South's struggle for independence.

The southern interest that might have been expected to make the greatest sacrifices for the cause was the interest for which many believed the war was being fought. But the slaveholding planters, taken as a group, were no more able to rise above narrow and selfish concerns than other segments of southern society. Because of their influence, the Confederacy was unable to adopt a sound financial policy; land and slaves, the main resources of the South, remained immune from direct taxes. As a result, the government was only able to raise about one percent of its revenue from taxation; the rest came from loans and the printing of vast quantities of fiat paper money. The inevitable consequence was the catastrophic runaway inflation that made Confederate money almost worthless even before the government went out of existence. Besides resisting the taxation of their wealth, planters fought bitterly against efforts to regulate what they raised on their land, battled and obstructed attempts to impress their food crops to meet the urgent needs of the Confederate commissary, and vehemently refused to cooperate in plans to make use of slaves for public purposes. Strong planter opposition to the impressment of slaves was a principal factor in the failure of the Confederacy to gain control over a third of its manpower. Had planters not feared the loss of immediate control over their bondsmen or suspected that they might be "damaged" in government service, the Confederacy could have drawn on a large pool of forced labor for the construction of railroads, the building of fortifications, and even the production of goods. One of the South's most damaging manpower shortages was the lack of sufficient factory workers, too many of whom had been drafted into the army. Slaves were not conscripted to fill this void despite the fact that prewar experience had provided ample evidence that slaves could be used successfully in manufacturing.[15] Without giving up slavery as an institution or taking the desperate gamble of arming blacks in the hope that they

[15] See Robert Starobin, *Industrial Slavery in the Old South* (New York, 1970).

would fight for the South, the Confederacy could have made substantial use of slaves as a flexible and mobile labor force capable of being allocated to those sectors of the war economy that most needed labor. As it was, planters kept too many of their slaves at home, where, because of a shortage of overseers and the impending approach of northern armies, they became increasingly unproductive and difficult to control. It was not devotion to slavery *per se* that accounts for this situation but rather a peculiarly limited and narrow-minded concept of slavery as an institution necessarily linked to agriculture and a plantation environment.

Southern particularism and rigidity were also manifested in the area of public safety and internal security. Although the South had a much more severe disloyalty problem than the North, Davis resorted to martial law and suspension of the writ of habeas corpus more sparingly than Lincoln. Unwilling to declare martial law on his own authority, as Lincoln had done, Davis awaited Congressional authorization which was given only reluctantly and in small doses. The Confederate President was allowed to suspend the writ during three brief periods totaling sixteen months and then only in limited geographical areas. As a result of this cautious use of executive power, Unionist guerrilla movements were able to thrive in the mountainous backcountry of the South, and large numbers of conscripts were released from military service by state judges who registered their belief in the unconstitutionality of the draft by freely issuing writs of habeas corpus to inductees. Thus, while the Lincoln administration was arresting and holding without trial thousands of allegedly disloyal northerners and also surpressing unfriendly newspapers, the Confederate government made little effort to counter even the most flagrant manifestations of dissent, divisiveness, and sedition. This contrast can scarcely be attributed to a greater southern devotion to civil liberties. Prewar critics of slavery had learned how narrow the limits of southern tolerance could be. The southern majority did not object to the forcible suppression of unpopular individuals, groups, and opinions, but its strong commitment to localism made it reluctant to see such powers exercised by a central government. In staunchly pro-Confederate areas, outright disloyalty could be dealt with by time-honored vigilante methods. But local pressures were unavailing against whole districts, such as portions of eastern Tennessee and western North Carolina, where a majority of the population had remained loyal to the Union.

Taking all the evidence into account, it seems safe to conclude that the South lost the war primarily because it had fewer sources of cohesion than the North and less aptitude for innovation. In political, economic, social, and even military spheres, the North demonstrated a greater capacity for organization and creative adaptation. The North fought the war progressively, readily making major adjustments and accepting new policies whenever change promised to bring results. The South fought on the whole regressively, learning little and compounding its errors. It was hampered and eventually defeated by a particularistic ethos that made it difficult and sometimes impossible for southerners to discard traditional habits and attitudes even when they were obviously detrimental to the cause.

The description of these behavioral patterns might seem to provide a sufficient answer to our initial question. But there is the further problem of explaining precisely why the North and South responded so differently to the challenges they faced. What was there about the culture and social structure of the North that made possible the kinds of organizational initiatives and daring innovations that have been described? What was there about southern society and culture that explains the lack of cohesiveness and adaptability that doomed the Confederacy? Answers to such questions require some further understanding of the differences in northern and southern society on the eve of the war, especially as these differences related to war-making potential.

A fuller comprehension of what social strengths and weaknesses the two sides brought to the conflict can perhaps be gained by borrowing a well-known concept from the social sciences—the idea of modernization. Sociologists and political scientists often employ this term to describe the interrelated changes that occur when a whole society begins to move away from a traditional agrarian pattern toward an urban-industrial system. There is a growing tendency, however, to see modernization as an open-ended and relative process rather than as the stereotyped evolution from one fixed state to another. According to this formulation, societies can be relatively modernized or nonmodernized, but there are no existing models of either perfect modernity, or, in recent history at least, of societies organized on a large scale that totally lack modernizing tendencies.[16]

---

[16] My understanding of modernization theory comes mainly from C. E. Black, *The Dynamics of Modernization: A Study in Comparative History* (New York, 1966); Marion J. Levy, Jr., *Modernization and the Structure of Societies* (Princeton, N.J., 1966); and S. N. Eisenstadt, *Modernization: Protest and Change* (Englewood Cliffs, N.J., 1966). On the value of relativistic approaches to modernization, see Levy, *Modernization*, pp. 12-14; and Anthony D. Smith, *Theories of Nationalism* (London, 1971), pp. 96-99.

One recent student of the subject describes the concept as follows:

Modernization . . . refers to the dynamic form that the age-old process of innovation has assumed as a result of the explosive proliferation of knowledge in recent centuries. It owes its special significance both to its dynamic character and to the universality of its impact on human affairs. It stems initially from an attitude, a belief that society can and should be transformed, that change is desirable. If a definition is necessary, "modernization" may be defined as the process by which historically evolved institutions are adapted to the rapidly changing functions that reflect the unprecedented increase in man's knowledge, permitting control over his environment, that accompanied the scientific revolution.[17]

Another theorist has provided a simple rule of thumb to gauge the extent of modernization in various societies: the higher the proportion of energy derived from inanimate sources, as opposed to the direct application of human and animal strength, the more modernized the society.[18] Modernization therefore has its intellectual foundations in a rationalistic or scientific world view and a commitment to technological development; it comes to fruition in the industrialization of production, the increase of the urban sector relative to the rural, the centralization or consolidation of political, social, and cultural activity, the recruitment of leadership on a basis of merit and efficiency rather than ascribed or hereditary characteristics, and the mobilization of the general population to serve collective ends as defined by a dominant elite.

By any definition of this process, the North was relatively more modernized than the South in 1861. To apply one of the most important indices of modernization, thirty-six percent of the Northern population was already urban as compared to the South's nine and six-tenths percent.[19] As we have already seen, there was an even greater gap in the extent of industrialization. Furthermore, the foundations had been laid in the northern states for a rapid increase in the pace of modernization. The antebellum "transportation revolution" had set the stage for economic integration on a national scale, and the quickening pace of industrial development foreshadowed the massive and diversified growth of

[17] Black, *Dynamics*, p. 7.

[18] Levy, *Modernization*, pp. 11-12.

[19] Ramondo Luraghi, "The Civil War and the Modernization of American Society: Social Structure in the Old South before and during the War," *Civil War History* XVIII (September 1972), p. 237.

the future. Because of better and cheaper transportation, new markets, and a rise in efficiency and mechanization, midwestern agriculture was in a position to begin playing its modern role as the food-producing adjunct to an urban-industrial society. Literacy was widespread and means of mass communication, such as inexpensively produced newspapers, pamphlets, and books, were available for mobilizing public opinion. The opening up of the political system and the increase of economic opportunities had made rapid social mobility possible, especially in newly developing areas, and had increased the chances that leadership would be based on achievement rather than social background. As the socioeconomic system became more complex, greater specialization of individual and institutional functions was occurring. Organizational skills, developed on the local level in small enterprises and in the numerous voluntary organizations that dominated community life, were ready to be tapped for larger tasks of national integration. In short, given the necessary stimulus and opportunity, the North was ready for a "great leap forward" in the modernization process.

The South, on the other hand, had little potentiality for rapid modernization. Overwhelmingly agricultural and tied to the slave plantation as its basic unit of production, it had many of the characteristics of what today would be called "an underdeveloped society." Like such societies, the Old South had what amounted to a "dual economy": a small modern or capitalistic sector, profitably producing cotton and other commodities for export, coexisted with a vast "traditional" sector, composed of white subsistence farmers and black slaves. The subsistence farmers had no role at all in the market economy, and slaves contributed to it only as a source of labor.[20] Compared with the North, the South relied much more heavily on animate sources of energy, especially the work of slaves using primitive implements. Without substantial urban, commercial, and industrial centers of its own, the southern economy was almost completely dependent on the outside world for the utilization of its products. Large-scale economic diversification and technological progress were inconceivable without revolutionary changes in its social and economic system.

Besides lacking the foundations for the kind of unified and self-sustaining modern economy that was developing in the North, the South was also characterized by a fragmented social order. Most ob-

[20] See Morton Rothstein, "The Antebellum South as a Dual Economy: A Tentative Hypothesis," *Agricultural History* XLI (October 1967), pp. 373-82.

vious was the radical disjunction between the conditions of life and fundamental interests of white masters and black slaves; but even among whites the dual economy was probably paralleled by something approaching a dual society. It is at least arguable that the outlook and way of life of the rich planters diverged significantly from the folk culture of the backcountry farmers who owned no slaves or only a few.[21] In the North—because of the growing interdependence and diffused prosperity caused by improved communications and market facilities—midwestern farmers, eastern manufacturers, and, to some extent at least, skilled artisans and industrial workers not only felt they had common interests but could also partake of a common culture rooted in the Protestant ethic. Central to their world view was the myth of equal and unlimited opportunity generated by a rapidly growing capitalistic economy in which gross and unfair differences in wealth and privilege had not yet become palpable. The two main segments of the white South were united neither by a sense of common economic interests nor by a complete identity of social and political values. But the presence of millions of black slaves did make possible a perverse kind of solidarity. Fear of blacks, and more specifically of black emancipation, was the principal force holding the white South together. Without it, there could have been no broadly based struggle for independence.[22]

The planter and the non-slaveholding farmer had one other characteristic in common besides racism; in their differing ways, they were both extreme individualists. The planter's individualism came mainly from a lifetime of commanding slaves on isolated plantations. Used to unquestioned authority in all things and prone to think of himself as an aristocrat, he commonly exhibited an indomitable sense of personal independence. The non-slaveholder, on the other hand, was basically a backwoodsman who combined the stiff-necked individualism of the frontier with the arrogance of race that provided him with an exaggerated sense of his personal worth. Southern whites in general therefore were conditioned by slavery, racism, and rural isolation to condone and

[21] Although Frank Owsley's *Plain Folk of the Old South* (Baton Rouge, 1949) has justifiably been criticized for its thesis that a large middle class of white farmers who were not part of the plantation economy was the dominant element in southern society, his findings can still be used to support the view that there was a distinct and viable white folk culture that was to some degree independent of the cultural dominance of the plantation and the planter class. (See especially pp. 90-132.)

[22] See George M. Fredrickson, *The Black Image in the White Mind: The Debate on Afro-American Character and Destiny, 1817-1914* (New York, 1971), pp. 58-70.

even encourage quasi-anarchic patterns of behavior that could not have been tolerated in a more modernized society with a greater need for social cohesion and discipline. W. J. Cash has provided a graphic description of this syndrome in *The Mind of the South:*

In focusing the old backcountry pride upon the ideas of the superiority to the Negro and the peerage of the white man, and thereby (fully in the masses, and in some basic way in the planters) divorcing it from the necessity for achievement, [this individualism] inevitably shifted emphasis back upon and lent new impulsion to the purely personal and puerile attitude which distinguishes the frontier outlook everywhere. And when to that was added the natural effect on the planters of virtually unlimited sway over their bondsmen, and the natural effect on the whites of the example of these planters, it eventuated in this: that the individualism of the plantation world would be one which, like that of the backcountry before it, would be far too concerned with the bald, immediate, unsupported assertion of the ego, which placed too great stress on the inviolability of personal whim, and was full of the chip-on shoulder swagger and brag of a boy—one, in brief, by which the essence was the boast, voiced or not, on the part of every southerner, that he could knock hell out of whoever dared cross him.[23]

Such an attitude was obviously incompatible with the needs of a modernizing society for cooperation and collective innovation. Furthermore, the divorce of status from achievement made it less likely that competent leaders and organizers would emerge. Particularism, localism, and extreme individualism were the natural outgrowth of the South's economic and social system. So was resistance to any changes that posed a threat to slavery and racial domination. A few southern spokesmen of the 1850's did call for collective action to diversify agriculture and promote industrialization. Most of them were militant southern nationalists, deeply committed to the preservation of slavery, who acknowledged the South's vulnerability in any struggle with the more developed North and perceived that the successful establishment of southern independence required a greater degree of modernization. More, specifically, they believed that slavery could be combined with urban, commercial, and industrial development.[24] But they probably underestimated the objective barriers to economic diversifi-

[23] Wilbur J. Cash, *The Mind of the South* (New York: 1960), p. 44.

[24] See Robert Royal Russel, *Economic Aspects of Southern Sectionalism* (Urbana, Ill., 1924), pp. 179-98. For a cogent expression of the proposition that an independent slaveholding South could and should embark on extensive modernization, see Edmund Ruffin, *Anticipations of the Future, To Serve as Lessons for the Present Time* (Richmond, Va., 1860), pp. 410-11.

cation and, in any case, made relatively little headway against
traditional southern attitudes.

In one category of modernization, it might appear that the
South had kept reasonably abreast of the North. If a characteristic
of modernizing societies is an increase in the actual or symbolic
participation of the general population in the political process,
then the upsurge of democratic activity among whites beginning in
the age of Jackson might be taken as a sign of southern
modernity. Yet southern politics, despite its high level of popular
involvement, remained largely the disorganized competition of
individual office seekers. Those who won elections usually did so
either because they were already men of weight in their communities or because they came off better than their rivals in face-to-face
contact with predominantly rural voters. In the North by 1861,
politics was less a matter of personalities and more an impersonal
struggle of well-organized parties. In urban areas, the rudiments of
the modern political machine could already be perceived.[25]

The fact that the South was economically, socially, and politically less "developed" or modernized than the North in 1861 may
not by itself fully explain why war had to come, but it does provide
a key to understanding why the war had to turn out the way it did.
The northern successes and southern failures recounted earlier were
not mysterious or accidental. They were predetermined largely by
the essential nature of the two societies. The Civil War, despite its
insurrectionary origins, rapidly took on the character of a conventional war between two independent nations. In such a war, a
relatively modernized society has certain inherent advantages over
a relatively undeveloped society. Since the essence of modernization is the acceptance of change as normal and desirable, it
follows that the more modernized party in a conflict will be more
likely to make radical adjustments and welcome innovations. It
can also apply its more highly developed technology to the
instruments of warfare. Its greater social mobility and emphasis on
achievement will bring to the fore more effective leaders, and its
more highly differentiated structure of social and occupational
roles will make possible a more efficient allocation of tasks.
Finally, and most significantly, its greater political and economic
integration gives it a superior ability to exert centralized control
over the mobilization of men and resources.

Such a model would appear to account for all or most of the

[25] For a discussion of the differences between northern and southern political
culture, see Nichols, *Blueprints*, pp. 187-89.

patterns of wartime behavior that have been described. But there is one possible objection to this explanation that must be confronted. Just as the stronger side, as measured in crude physical terms, has not always won in wars of national independence, neither has the more modernized society always emerged triumphant. The recent American experience in Viet Nam provides fresh and dramatic evidence of this possibility. But the war in Viet Nam was essentially a guerrilla war; whenever the Viet Cong attempted to engage in conventional warfare, it was relatively unsuccessful. Had the South chosen at some point to change from conventional to guerrilla warfare, it might have stood a better chance of wearing down the North and gaining its independence. In partisan or guerrilla conflicts, the advantages of relative modernization are greatly diminished. The Anglo-Boer War of 1899-1902 might be taken as a case in point. The Boers, with their lack of advanced technology and their relatively primitive social and economic system, were no match for the British on the battlefield. After the conventional war was over, however, less than 40,000 Boer guerrillas were able to hold their own for two years against British forces eventually numbering half a million and possessing a much greater technological superiority than the North ever enjoyed in the Civil War. In order to win, the British had to scorch the countryside and intern a large proportion of the Afrikaner population.[26] The South, despite a greater physical capability than the Boers to engage in extensive guerilla warfare, chose not to do so. Perhaps southern nationalism was made of less stern stuff than that of the Afrikaners. But a more likely explanation for the southerners' refusal to revert to partisan war was their awareness of what effects such a policy would have on their social system. Above all things, southerners feared loss of control over the black population; their ultimate nightmare was a black uprising or "race war." To accept the inevitable chaos and disorder of a guerrilla war was also to accept the end of effective white supremacy. And this was something that white southerners were unwilling to contemplate even after the end of slavery itself had become inevitable.[27]

[26] N. C. Pollock and Swanzie Agnew, *An Historical Geography of South Africa* (London, 1963), pp. 196-200.

[27] The Boers, of course, had their own stake in white supremacy and feared loss of control over the African population in their republics and on the borders. But the Anglo-Boer War was fought only after the British and Afrikaners had crushed all major black resistance in southern Africa and was conducted on the basis of a "gentlemen's agreement" between Europeans that African intervention would not be permitted on

As it was, the only course open to southern leaders during the war was in effect a crash program of modernization in an attempt to neutralize the immense advantages of the North. When we consider the cultural heritage and economic resources they had to work with, their achievements went beyond what might have been expected.[28] But the South had far too much ground to make up, and persisting rigidities, especially as manifested in the die-hard commitment to localism, racism, and plantation slavery, constituted fatal checks on the modernizing impulse.

The North, on the other hand, not only capitalized on its initial advantages during the war but was able to multiply them. In fact, the conflict itself served as a catalyst for rapid development in many areas. Modernizing trends that had begun in the prewar period came to unexpectedly rapid fruition in a way that both compounded the North's advantage in the conflict and helped set the pattern for postwar America. The war saw the transformation of the federal government into a modern state, with a new revenue structure based partly on direct taxation, a national currency and banking system, the first active involvement of government agencies in the promotion of agriculture and technology, and the increased bureaucracy that all this entailed. Most significantly, the national government, through protective tariffs, subsidies, and land grants, began to play a more positive role in economic development. In the private sphere, the war gave impetus to the organization of business, philanthropy, and the professions on a broader scale. Hence the very tendencies toward consolidation and integration that gave the North a decisive advantage at the outset of the Civil War were accelerated by the exigencies and opportunities of the conflict. The very situation that led to northern victory made it possible for the war to propel the nation into a new and more advanced stage of modernization.

either side. (See David Denoon, *Southern Africa Since 1800* [New York and Washington, 1972], pp. 100-108.) During the American Civil War, no similar understanding was observed. The North's emancipation policy and use of black troops directly threatened the South's racial order and had implications for the conduct of the war that helped rule out partisan resistance. Ramondo Luraghi has also drawn attention to the South's peculiar reluctance to engage in guerrilla warfare in comparing the Civil War with the southern Italian peasants' rebellion against unification ("The Civil War and Modernization," pp. 246-247).

[28] These achievements are recounted in Emory Thomas' provocative book, *The Confederacy as a Revolutionary Experience* (Englewood Cliffs, N.J., 1971). In my opinion, however, Thomas greatly exaggerates the creative innovations and adaptations of the Confederacy and ignores a mass of evidence demonstrating rigid conservatism and inflexibility.

WILLIAM R. BROCK

Reconstruction
and the American Party System

THE BREAKDOWN OF THE NATIONAL two-party system in the decade before the Civil War is generally accepted as a symptom if not a cause of the catastrophe of 1861. The two old parties had been organized in every state of the Union; neither had been sectional, and both had offered voters real alternatives at every level of political life. The restoration of such a system was a natural objective once the Union had been preserved, and it was an unhappy legacy of Reconstruction that one party remained predominantly sectional while the other came to operate a one-party system in the South. The damage done to the Republican party by its failure to establish an effective southern wing is obvious; less apparent but nonetheless unfortunate was the irony of events which harnessed Jeffersonian traditions to southern conservatism.

If a national two-party system were to be established during the Reconstruction period, the initiative would have to come from the Republicans. It was their party which had no southern organization and theirs which had to convince enough southerners that the men who had been foremost in condemning their section nevertheless offered positive advantages for southern men. The major part of this essay will consider what chance the Republicans had of achieving this objective and in particular the possibility of creating a white Republican following in the South. Nevertheless, the Democrats also had a problem, and, in 1865, their future as a national party was by no means certain. In the South, conservatives, former Whigs, and states' rights Democrats of 1861 had little for which to thank northern Democrats, and it could not be assumed that former Democratic organizations would revive with new strength to restore the old alliance. And success in this quarter, if it came, might jeopardize their prospects with War Democrats and moderate Union men in the North. It is therefore appropriate to consider briefly the Democratic problem before turning to a more detailed examination of Republican prospects.

In 1866, Thurlow Weed, who had more experience than any other man in the art of political management, observed that

If the Democracy could, by its experience in adversity, learn that it could restore itself to popular confidence by *becoming loyal*, a reformed Democracy would ultimately recover possession of the Government.[1]

The prophecy might seem a bold one in the year when the Democrats suffered a disastrous defeat in the Congressional and state elections, but the facts supported it. In 1864, with many war Democrats endorsing Lincoln, the party had won 1,803,737 votes in the Union states, which was only 31,000 less than their *national* total in 1856. In New York, Lincoln's majority was less than 7,000, or under one percent of the votes cast. In Pennsylvania, he came safely home with a majority of 19,000, but even this was less than four percent of the poll. In his own Midwest, Lincoln had scored impressive victories—with majorities of 60,000 in Ohio, over 19,000 in Indiana, and over 30,000 in Illinois—but Union Democrats and the soldiers' vote had made significant contributions, and there might be a sharp reversal of the tide in future elections. If the Democrats could pick up even a part of their prewar southern vote in a reconstructed Union, their prospects as a national party looked bright, and the omens looked reasonably good if one studied the 1864 results in the slave states of the Union. Kentucky was a disaster for the Republicans, with a Democratic victory of more than two to one. Missouri was equally disastrous for the Democrats, with this former stronghold of their party going heavily Republican, while West Virginia celebrated her newfound independence by returning a large Republican majority. In Missouri, however, the poll was 60,000 down on the 1860

[1] As reported in the *New York Daily Tribune*, October 10, 1866. By this time Weed, following his friend Seward, was supporting Johnson and had endorsed the Democratic candidate for the governorship in New York.

figure, and no one could forecast what might happen when the boys in the Confederate armies came home. The Democrats won Delaware narrowly and lost Maryland by fewer than 2,000 in a low poll with the soldiers' vote holding the balance.

In the arithmetic of the Electoral College, the Democrats might therefore expect to win thirty-three in New York and could be reasonably optimistic (given a normal swing of the political pendulum and the return of Union Democrats to their former party) about twenty-one in Ohio, sixteen in Illinois, and thirteen in Indiana. The Union states on the border would yield thirty-two, and the states of the Confederacy fifty-nine. This would make a majority of the 1860 figure, and there might be a bonus from the Pacific states to make up for unexpected losses in the North. It is well known that these calculations came remarkably close to realization in 1868, when Grant's victory in the Electoral College was overwhelming, but the Democrats did remarkably well in the popular vote and seemed to demonstrate that their party was once more in fighting trim and nationwide in its organization. Given the revival in 1868 and these prospects for the future, the question is not why the Democrats did well but why they did not do much better. The Democrats did not win Illinois or Indiana until 1892, and then quickly lost them. Ohio remained faithful to the Republicans, and so did Pennsylvania. Only in New York did they find some reward, but even there the state remained marginal and changed hands at each successive election from 1868 to 1892. The Democrats did better in state than in national elections and better in congressional than in presidential elections; but even so, their results were disappointing when their opponents should have been losing momentum. In 1876, they might have won if full justice had been done, but would have depended upon the southern vote as they did in 1884 and 1892.

In the North, it was precisely this dependence upon the South that prejudiced the chances of Democratic success. As Thurlow Weed observed, to win the Democrats had to "become loyal," but their southern policy remained repugnant to a large number of northern men. As events had transpired, the northern Democrats did not lay down the terms to their southern colleagues; it was the southerners who dictated the conditions on which they would continue to support the party. Not every Democrat approved the doctrine of white supremacy when it meant systematic evasion of the law and the Constitution; a good many had a traditional distrust of southern upper-class rule; yet whatever their reservations, the national leaders had either to defend the record of their party in the South or simply pretend that unpleasant things had not happened. When Republican orators "waved the bloody shirt," they were not merely exploiting memories of the war; they were reminding northern voters of what was actually going on in the South.

The dependence of the Democrats upon the South had even more debilitating effects. It prevented them from evolving any coherent or constructive policies to meet the problems of an expanding and changing society. The Democratic party remained a party of negations, and most of the time their leaders could not agree upon what to deny. They depended in the North upon picking up a protest vote when times were hard; they had little to offer the work force of the new industrial society, and—despite their support among the foreign born, low-paid city dwellers, and farmers—they had no policies for urban America or depressed agriculture. It was left to the minority movements—to Green-backers, Grangers, Farmers' Alliances, Knights of Labor, and Populists—to diagnose the problems of the age and propose remedies.

There were other reasons why the Democrats failed to emerge as the majority party of the late nineteenth century. Their leadership was usually inferior to that of the Republicans, who, with all their errors, produced a remarkable breed of able and vigorous men. The conservatism of the Democrats did not appeal to the conservatism of business, despite the inclusion in their ranks of several wealthy bankers and merchants. Nor could the party which became deeply involved in the scandals of the Tweed ring and other city machines claim to be the party of pure government, although the Republicans outdid them in some cities and the Democrats gained from some highly publicized national scandals. A vital weakness of the Democrats in the North was their failure to capture the intellectuals; some writers (such as Mark Twain in *The Gilded Age*) were critical of all public life, but by and large the ablest editors, best-known authors, most prominent ministers of religion, and a majority of college professors stuck to the Republican party. In spite of all its blemishes, it remained for them the representative in America of all the liberal and enlightened ideas of the age. This failure of Democrats to appeal to the makers of opinion—particularly of educated opinion—was a far more serious deficiency than is sometimes imagined and can be attributed mainly to the party's role in the one-party South.

If the Democrats missed opportunities in the North, it is clear that the Republicans failed in the South. Yet in the early stages of the Reconstruction, their leaders were surprisingly optimistic about their prospects. Again and again they argued from the premise that new leadership would emerge if only the secessionists were excluded from public life and that the new men would be ready and willing to hold out the hand of fellowship to the Republicans. This expectation was based on the belief that secession had always been a minority movement, that the true men of the South had been Unionist at heart, and that even those who had been deluded were now so thoroughly disgusted with the traditional ruling class that they would seize power as soon as the opportunity offered. Thus the southern Republican party already existed in limbo and simply required some encouragement and protection in the initial stages to organize a majority. Though some Republicans supported black suffrage from an early stage, the majority did not do so; their hopes were based on the prospects for a white southern Republican movement, and part of their discontent with Andrew Johnson's policy was that he prevented this apparently natural development. It was perhaps paradoxical that much of the evidence for this belief came from Tennessee, where Johnson, as military governor, had built upon a solid base of white Unionism, and the subsequent domination of the state by his bitter personal enemy, William G. Brownlow, merely demonstrated to Republicans that the southern people would prove to be more radical than the President if only they were allowed their head.

Even more powerful than the belief that southern whites would repudiate their former leaders was the conviction that the Republican party embodied principles of such self-evident merit that even former enemies must acknowledge them. A typical statement (by an untypical Republican) was that of Benjamin F. Butler when he proclaimed that "The people believe the Republican party has saved the country; they believe that it desires to maintain liberty and free institutions secured by law, that in spite of all its mistakes and its shortcomings and all its sins of omission and commission—and they are many, to our shame be it spoken—that the interests of the country, . . . as an exemplar for mankind, are safer in the hands of the Republican party than in the hands of that Democracy who sympathised with the rebellion and threaten when in power to unsettle the issues closed by war."[2] The faith in their own destiny

[2] *The Present Relation of Parties* (Boston, 1870); being the reprint of a speech made by Butler at Boston, November 23, 1869.

was a source of tremendous strength in the North but made it difficult for Republicans to grasp that their version of the truth was not self-evident in the South.

When, following upon Johnson's plan of Reconstruction, former Confederates of the old ruling class were chosen for office, the Republicans saw not only a blow to their political prospects but also the threatened defeat of a social, political, and intellectual revolution in the South. They had hoped that not only the mass of the southern white people, but also entrepreneurs of a new type—commercial and industrial, northern newcomer and native southerner—would see the ruin of a discredited "aristocracy" as an opportunity to create a society which would recognize its community of interest with the North. The instrument for this reconstruction of southern society would be the southern wing of the Republican party, and it was this fair prospect that Johnson's hasty "restoration" put in jeopardy. We know that Republican hopes were not fulfilled, and many would argue that they never had a chance of fulfillment. Nevertheless, it is worthwhile to weigh up the odds, and, when this has been done, it may be concluded that the prospects of reviving a national two-party system were not so illusory as hindsight may suggest.

The minds of many Republicans naturally turned back to the days when northern and southern men had cooperated in the Whig party. Broadly speaking, there had been three types of southern Whig constituency. The first was in the cotton belt dominated by wealthy planters; the second was in the few commercial centers; and the third was in the backcountry or Appalachian valleys where there were few or no slaves and many small farmers. The first type might be regarded as lost since most Whig planters had supported the Confederacy, though a few consistent Unionists might be found among them. In the commercial cities, the Republicans hoped for more positive response, and even former secessionists might be ready to reinforce economic interest by political affiliation with northern friends. In the North, merchants, bankers, railroad men, and textile manufacturers were only too eager to hold out the hand of fellowship.[3] There had been an enormous prewar investment in the trade and markets of the South, and the

[3] Much work remains to be done on the intricate pattern of economic relationships which existed between the sections before 1861. Secessionist rhetoric stressed tension and separation, but northern merchants and southern planters (particularly those sending their produce to distant markets and dependent upon northern credit) were the strongest supporters of compromise. During the Reconstruction years, the commercial magnates of New York were among the strongest supporters of Andrew Johnson. Their advance agents arrived in southern cities as soon as the fighting ended. There was intense

opportunities for the future were enormous. The *New York Times*, which appealed particularly to more conservative northern businessmen, preached the doctrine that political harmony would follow naturally upon the restoration of good economic relations. In May 1866, it quoted with approval a statement from the Richmond *Dispatch* that "The paralysis of the South can but cripple and impede the North. . . . The crippling of that South which furnished two-thirds of the exports of the United States before the war cannot but impair the National wealth and seriously diminish its resources."[4] A week later the *Times* gave prominence to a southern railroad president's assertion that "Every material interest at the North and West is much concerned in the rapid restoration of Southern industry."[5] Later in the year, the *Times* still hoped that the mutual benefits of economic association would overcome sectional antipathies; northern capital was "prayed for" in the South; northern men were invited so that valueless land could become profitable; and "Northern enterprise is called upon to extend its ramifications southwards that home wants may be supplied, and places now desolate become scenes of thrifty labor."[6]

Horace Greeley's rival and radical *Tribune* was equally emphatic about the need for economic integration to offset the divisions engendered by war. In June 1866, northern men who engaged in cotton planting were assured of excellent prospects, and there were many districts in which men would be welcome if they came "with capital and industry to cultivate the soil." Less endowed but hard-working men could also expect to do well, since the end of slavery had completely dispelled the idea that white men could not toil in the southern climate.[7] The protectionist *Tribune* also noted with satisfaction that southern newspapers recorded enthusiastically the establishment of new factories and foundries, while opposition to duties on imported manufacturing had completely disappeared.[8]

Northern merchants were anxious to pick up the threads, and

---

competition, not only between the eastern cities but also between them and the river cities of the Ohio and upper Mississippi valleys, to penetrate southern markets. This economic drive to recover southern markets and foster southern revival was likely to support any political solution which could guarantee social stability and encourage private enterprise.

[4] *New York Times*, May 21, 1866.

[5] *Ibid.*, May 28, 1866, quoting John P. King.

[6] *Ibid.*, November 1, 1866.

[7] *New York Tribune*, June 7, 1866.

[8] *Ibid.*, November 27, 1866.

Massachusetts merchants and manufacturers joined with William King of Georgia to use their considerable influence at Washington to ensure that the Freedmen's Bureau Bill of 1866 included a provision enabling the Bureau to organize labor on the plantations.[9] "If three million bales of cotton are made this year," stated the *Tribune*, "the Freedmen's Bureau will have given us at least one third of it, worth not less than $100,000 in gold."[10] In the South, there was an implicit realization that recovery could come only with the aid of northern capital, enterprise, and technical skill, while behind the scenes many upper-class southerners were busy seeking just these things to restore their own fortunes and to bring about an economic revolution.

The difficulty was that Republicans looked south with two faces. They hoped for cooperation with the economic leaders of the South while seeking to deprive them of political authority, and worked for accord in harnessing the upper class to the Union government by ties of economic interest while destroying their political leadership. Many Republicans failed to understand the contradiction and continued to talk as though southern Unionism could fill both roles. In contrast, President Johnson hoped for a popular mandate but was driven into alliance with the upper class and commercial wealth of the South. By the late summer of 1866, with crucial congressional elections on the way, Republicans were forced to decide the national future of their party. The path marked out by Johnson was an alliance between conservative Republicans, War Democrats, and the southern upper class. This was the essential heart of the National Union movement which endorsed the President's policies in the Philadelphia Convention of August 1866, and no one was more active in attempting to win over the bulk of the Republican party to this plan of action than Henry J. Raymond, editor of the *New York Times* and chairman of the Republican National Executive Committee.

On June 18, 1866, Raymond delivered a speech in Congress which was intended as a rallying call for Republicans who sought to nationalize their party on these lines. There must, he said, be "a National instead of a Sectional party." If the Republican leadership persisted in their course, the northern Democrats might

[9] Details are given by George R. Woolfolk, *The Cotton Regency: the Northern Merchants and Reconstruction* (New York, 1958), pp. 47-52, 69-75. I do not agree with Mr. Woolfolk's political interpretation, but his work contains a great deal of valuable information about the efforts of northern merchants to reestablish their southern trade.

[10] February 20, 1866. Quoted in Woolfolk, *Cotton Regency,* p. 214, n. 61.

combine after the next elections with southern representatives designate and claim to be the true Congress representing a majority of the nation. Raymond admitted that Republicans had reasonable grounds for refusing to associate with Clement Vallandigham or Fernando Wood, but the Philadelphia convention offered a forum in which Republicans could seek an understanding with the sound men of the South.[11] In his newspaper, Raymond insisted in a sentence that could have been inspired from the White House that President Johnson "desired above all things to have a Union party of the whole country, supported in the North as well as in the South." He went on to say that, if the opportunity were missed, the Republican party might be short-lived despite its achievements.

A political party, like the ice of a frozen lake, melts away from beneath, and while at evening its surface may seem to be perfectly solid and untouched by rift or seam, the breeze of a single night may perfect the work which weeks of silent and unseen decay have been preparing.[12]

At a Republican caucus in Washington on July 10, Raymond argued that the Philadelphia meeting would not destroy but strengthen the Union party, since a dependable Southern wing was essential for its future existence. Congressional leadership thought otherwise. Alliance with a revived upper class would sacrifice the two groups upon whom Republicans knew that they could depend and to whom they were morally committed—Unionists and freedmen—and this logic inspired the caucus resolution moved by Thaddeus Stevens that "no one who favored the Philadelphia convention could have any fellowship with the Union party." Against this resolution only one negative vote was cast (Raymond himself not voting).[13] This was decisive. Raymond continued to protest that "there was a distinct understanding that the meeting at Philadelphia of Republicans and Democrats did not involve any essential change in the ordinary party relations of either," but the facts were against him.[14] No Republican who attended the convention after the caucus vote could be regarded by the leader-

[11] *New York Times*, June 18, 1866. This report differs in some respects from the speech as printed in the *Congressional Globe*; the latter does not include the fanciful remark that Johnson might recognize the Democrats and southern representatives as the legally constituted Congress.

[12] *New York Times*, May 29, 1866.

[13] *Ibid.*, September 3, 1866.

[14] *Ibid.*, September 7, 1866.

ship as a member of a party in good standing, and, in this deliber-
ate manner, the Congressional party had rejected one method by
which they could win southern support.

This decision might have been reversed if the congressional
elections of 1866 had revealed the weaknesses predicted by
Raymond; instead, they proved to be a triumph for the party
which had so solidly opposed the President, passed the Civil Rights
Act, extended the life and powers of the Freedmen's Bureau, and
approved the Fourteenth Amendment. Even if these positive
achievements did not persuade the voters, the New Orleans riot
and killing on July 30, 1866, caused a profound impression and
helped to discredit the restored governments in northern eyes.
Andrew Johnson's unprecedented intervention in congressional
elections was also unfortunate for his cause, and the attitude he
displayed was even more damaging than his loss of dignity. Even
the *New York Times* admitted that it had been "a great mistake
on the part of the President to assume or to suppose that the great
body of the people in the North who dissent from his views, are
enemies of the Union or are seeking consciously to destroy it" and
"that the mere suspicion of affiliation with the Copperhead
element suffered to counteract all the influence of the Administration."[15] Finally, the President's attempts to use federal patronage
appeared to demonstrate that faithful party men were to be sacri-
ficed to appease secessionists. Senator Sherman asserted that every
officeholder in Ohio had been requested to attend the Philadelphia
convention or explain his reasons for not doing so and had been
told to contribute towards "the support of a new party in
antagonism to the party that brought the President into power and
to which they were attached." He said that nearly every prominent officeholder had been dismissed, and their replacements had
been nominated by "self-constituted committees . . . organized to
supervise the distribution of the federal patronage."[16] General
Schenck, also of Ohio, said (with some exaggeration) that "never
in the whole history of this country has there been any party so
purely a mere bread-and-butter brigade as these creatures who had
crawled into office within the last year."[17] These breaches of the
normal rules for the distribution of patronage through party
channels meant that the people of a district often had visible proof
that Johnson's policy meant the replacement of respected political

[15] *Ibid.*, November 23, 1866.
[16] *Congressional Globe*, 39 Congress, 2 session, p. 43, January 16, 1867.
[17] *Congressional Globe*, 39 Congress, 2 session, p. 373, January 9, 1867.

veterans by men who (to quote Schenck) "do not pretend to have any principles." If southern friends and good northern Republicans were to be betrayed, who would remain to form a true party of national union?

It was estimated that in 1866 the twenty free states gave the Republicans a majority of 405,000 where Lincoln had had 395,000 including the soldiers' vote. The Republican majorities were larger in the states which polled in November than those which polled in October, and states with the highest polls gave to Republicans the biggest majorities. The Republicans also did very well where governorships were at stake. Maine gave Governor Chamberlain a majority of 28,000; in Pennsylvania, John W. Geary scored a victory over Heister Clymer; in New York, Reuben Fenton beat John Hoffman by more than 14,000, despite endorsement of the Democrat by Thurlow Weed. In Connecticut, General Joseph Hawley beat the popular and experienced James English. The results in large marginal states were particularly encouraging for the Republicans. They elected sixteen Congressmen in Ohio against three Democrats; eighteen against six in Pennsylvania; all but three seats in Indiana; all the seats in Michigan and all but one in Wisconsin. In New Jersey, where Democrats had long had the advantage, both houses of the legislature went Republican. In the fortieth Congress, the party score would stand at 143 to 49.

The results of the election were easily assessed. Many years later, James G. Blaine explained that "the Republicans plainly saw that the triumph of President Johnson meant a triumph of the Democratic party under an alias . . . [and] that the same political combination which had threatened the destruction of the Union would be recalled to its control."[18] *The New York Times* asserted that "seldom . . . has a contest been conducted with so exclusive a reference to a single issue" and argued that the South must accept the verdict and the President concede the point.[19] The *New York Tribune* quoted advice from the *Chicago Times* to the Democrats to cut adrift from Johnson's administration, cease being a "holdback" or "conservative" party, and become what it had been in its palmy days, a progressive and aggressive party.[20] There seemed to be little likelihood that the advice would be taken.

[18] James G. Blaine, *Twenty Years of Congress: From Lincoln to Garfield.* (2 vols. Norwich, Conn., 1884-86). II, p. 243.

[19] *New York Times,* October 11, 1866 (written after results in the "October states" were announced).

[20] *New York Tribune,* November 14, 1866 (from *Chicago Times,* November 12).

Fresh from this triumph it was unlikely that the Republicans would embrace the National Union solution, and they turned naturally towards southern Unionism, Negro suffrage, and a political revolution which would transform southern society. Months before, Horace Greeley had written in the *New York Tribune*:

No matter what a few prominent men may say, the North is eager to shake hands with the South and forget all that ever divided them. The chief obstacle to this is the determination evidenced by those who monopolize power in the South to keep the Blacks forever in vassalage, and thus prescribe and trample on those Whites who have been always for the Union.[21]

This association between the rights of blacks and the white Unionism had made little headway during the spring and summer because the politicians feared commitment to political equality between the races; yet by the fall, its logic was becoming apparent even among midwestern Republicans who had hitherto been the most reluctant to discuss the question. In Indiana, George W. Julian found a readiness to discuss Negro suffrage during the 1866 campaign and increasing support for it.

A great national emergency pleaded for it. . . . The question involved the welfare of both races, and the issue of the war. It involved not merely the fate of the negro but the safety of society.[22]

Years later, James G. Blaine wrote of "an unmistakable manifestation throughout the whole political canvass of 1866, by the more advanced section of the Republican party, in favor of demanding impartial suffrage as the basis for reconstruction in the South" and added that the impulse "came from the people rather than the political leaders."[23] Politicians who had favored Negro suffrage seem to have been feeling their way until the results of the elections were known; they were then encouraged to go forward. In a speech at Bedford, Pennsylvania, on September 4, 1866, Thaddeus Stevens said,

The great issue to be met at the election is the question of negro rights. I shall

[21]*New York Tribune*, February 12, 1866.
[22]George W. Julian, *Political Recollections, 1840 to 1872*. Reprint of 1884 ed., p. 264.
[23]Blaine, *Twenty Years of Congress*, II. pp. 243-44.

not deny, but admit, that a fundamental principle of the Republican creed is that every being possessed of an immortal soul is equal before the law.[24]

However, at Lancaster a few days later, he was more cautious, saying that Negroes lacked education and would be too easily led by their former masters, and, in December, he submitted a bill for the government of North Carolina which included only limited Negro suffrage. Yet at the same time, he was saying that the people had shown themselves to be in advance of Congress and that Republicans must move forward to get abreast of public opinion. The decision of the Supreme Court in *Ex Parte Milligan* seems to have decided the issue for him; the ballot must be extended as soon and as far as possible to provide the protection hitherto afforded by the military courts.[25]

James A. Garfield, who was never the most ardent of radicals, believed that if the southern states accepted the Fourteenth Amendment, Congress was morally bound to admit them; but, if they rejected it, impartial suffrage must follow.[26] Senator Gratz Brown from Missouri made an emphatic declaration in favor of impartial suffrage on December 12, 1866. He attacked the theory, fashionable among conservatives, that "this right of franchise [was] only a conventional or political arrangement that may be abrogated at will . . . a privilege yielded to you and I and others by society or the government which represents society." He went on to quote Herbert Spencer's maxim that the source of all rights was "the liberty of each individual limited by the like liberty of all," and concluded that "any recognition of an inequality of rights is fatal to liberty."[27] John A. Bingham, although opposed to making suffrage "a perpetual and fundamental condition" for the ad-

[24] Stevens Papers, Library of Congress.

[25] A criticism of this interpretation of the 1866 election has been made by Lawrence A. Powell, "Rejected Republican Incumbents in the 1866 Congressional Nominating Conventions," *Civil War History* 19 (September 1973), pp. 221-327. He examines a small number of instances in which sitting Republicans were denied renomination, and finds that personal and factional issues, not Reconstruction policies, were at stake. He argues that "surely one area where national influence on northern politics ought to have been reflected was in those Congressional districts which denied renomination to an aspiring Republican incumbent." This is untenable when a party was so united in its policy. It would be true only if a supporter of Johnson had been involved in the contest. The most prominent Johnson Republican—Henry J. Raymond—did not seek renomination after assessing his chances in New York.

[26] Mary A. Hinsdale (ed.), *Garfield-Hinsdale Letters* (Ann Arbor, Mich., 1949), p. 88; Theodore C. Smith, *Life and Letters of James A. Garfield* (New Haven, Conn., 1925). I, pp. 396-97.

[27] *Congressional Globe,* 39 Congress, 2 session, p. 76.

mission of Nebraska, nevertheless hoped that the time was coming when "manhood, fidelity to the law, and citizenship shall be the only test of suffrage or eligibility for office."[28]

Historians hostile to the Republicans have therefore been correct in seeing the establishment of a Republican base in the South as a motive for making impartial suffrage a condition of Reconstruction, although their inferences owe more to racial prejudice than evidence. The Republicans hoped that their party would become national; alliance with the upper class at the expense of the Unionists and freedmen would have been an abandonment of principle; now it was logical to bring in new voters to balance the old. What is often overlooked, by both critics and apologists, is that the Republican leaders never intended to depend upon the black vote alone. The census statistics were sufficient to demonstrate that no party could maintain itself in the South without white votes, and it was to the lower and middle classes of southern white society that Republicans looked for support and from whom they expected new leaders to undertake the reconstruction of southern society. The truly interesting question is, therefore, the extent to which these Republican hopes rested upon dream or reality.

The best hunting grounds for white southern Republican votes were the southern counties with large white majorities which had been predominantly Whig between 1840 and 1852 or nourished the traditions of Jacksonian nationalism. In 1852, at the lowest point in their fortunes, the Whigs had received about 295,500 votes in the eleven states which subsequently joined the Confederacy. In addition, they had won 128,800 in the four slave states which remained in the Union.[29] The Republicans might also hope to secure Democratic counties where Unionism had remained alive during the war. In addition to popular support in these areas, the Republicans hoped to win over former Whigs of the upper class who had opposed secession.

[28] *Congressional Globe*, 39 Congress, 2 session, p. 451, January 14, 1867. Both Gratz and Bingham were arguing for impartial suffrage in all states and not in the South alone.

[29] For population figures and racial distribution in the following pages, the census of 1860 has been used. This, of course, understated most figures as they were in 1868, but was the latest census available to those who wished to indulge in electoral calculations. In estimating the proportion between the races, the 1860 census is probably a more reliable guide in southern states than that of 1870. For election figures in presidential elections, by state and county, all references are to W. Dean Burnham, *Presidential Ballots 1836-1892* (Baltimore, 1955). Figures in this and the next paragraph are given to the nearest 1,000. South Carolina is not included in the figures for 1852 as there was no direct election for presidential electors before 1868.

The test came in the presidential election of 1868. In seven former Confederate states, 404,700 Republican votes were cast, and the four Union slave states, together with West Virginia, yielded 193,400.[30] In the lower South, the large majority of Republican votes came from the plantation counties where blacks were numerous, but, in the upper South, the picture was much more varied.

The 1868 result in North Carolina was encouraging for the Republicans. Grant carried the state with substantial support from white Unionists fighting hard for political survival. In 1865, they had cast 25,809 votes for a Unionist governor, although the Democrats won with 32,539. In 1866, the Unionist vote for governor dropped to 10,794, but it was said that many had abstained because the candidate was personally unpopular.[31] The census of 1860 had recorded 629,942 whites or approximately 120,000 adult males; the proportion of votes cast for governor in 1865 suggested that on a full poll these might divide into 65,000 Democrats and 56,000 Unionists. There were 361,522 blacks in 1860, which might mean 72,000 adult male votes after enfranchisement. This underestimates the figures for 1868 but provides a useful guideline. Immediately after the passage of the first Reconstruction Act, the Unionists called for a constitutional convention and unanimously accepted Negro suffrage.[32]

Ten days later, the *New York Tribune* recorded its satisfaction that "for the first time in the history of the State, colored men will be recognized as the political equals of the white men,"[33] and North Carolina was thus the exemplar of Republican hopes for the nationalization of their party. In the election, 181,499 votes were cast of which 96,939 were Republican and 84,560 Democrat; the turnout was over 84,000 more than in 1860. This suggests that

[30] South Carolina (where 62,000 Republican votes were cast) is included. Virginia, Florida, Mississippi, and Texas were not yet restored to the Union. There has been considerable controversy over the social status and political antecedents of Southern "scalawags" (c.f. David Donald in *Journal of Southern History* x (1944), 447-60; Thomas B. Alexander, *ibid.*, xxi 305-29; Alan W. Trelease, *ibid.*, xxix. 445-68; Richard L. Hume, *ibid.*, xxxix. 183 ff.). One may get a different answer if one is looking for leaders or voters. I accept the argument by Trelease that "the great majority of native white Republicans . . . were hill-country farmers . . . affiliation with the Radicals was a natural resumption of their earlier political outlook." I agree with Donald and Alexander that there were more former Whigs than Democrats in the Republican party in the South, but Hume's study of Arkansas shows how men of this social category turned to Republicanism even when they previously been strongly Democratic.

[31] *New York Tribune*, March 9, 1867.

[32] *Ibid.*, Same date.

[33] *Ibid.*, March 19, 1867.

about 20,000 former white Unionists joined the Democrats, while about 25,000 remained to constitute a Republican majority with some 70,000 new black voters. This hypothesis is supported by an examination of the county returns which show the formerly Whig "white" counties dividing between Republicans and Democrats, while the Republicans carried most counties in which there were large black minorities.

The Republicans won forty-six counties in North Carolina against forty-three for the Democrats. Of the thirty-two counties with large black minorities, the Republicans won twenty-two and the Democrats ten. In some counties, the black vote could have been decisive but only if the white vote was divided. The Republicans also won three counties in which there were black majorities. A marked feature was, however, Republican success in nineteen counties in which there were large white majorities; and though the Democrats won thirty other "white" counties, the vote was very close in eleven and indicated the presence of a powerful Republican challenge. In the future, Republicans might hope to carry some of these marginal counties, and a high poll meant that there were no hidden reserves of Democratic voters to swing the pendulum.

Arkansas was another state in which affairs looked auspicious for southern Republicanism. Grant won twenty-four counties against twenty-two for the Democrats. Of the twenty-four Republican counties, sixteen were "white" counties and four more had white majorities of more than two to one. Three Republican counties had large black minorities, but in two of them high polls indicated that some whites voted Republican. In only one county was there a black majority. Arkansas had been overwhelmingly Democratic before the war, so in this state the Republicans drew their principal support from former Democratic nationalists of the white counties. Most counties voting Republican in 1868 had voted for Breckinridge in 1860, but this had demonstrated their loyalty to the regular Democratic ticket rather than an enthusiasm for secession. Thus Arkansas illustrated precisely the kind of popular upsurge that Republicans hoped to enlist in their cause.

The position was different in Tennessee. The state had its own drastic restrictions on voting by ex-Confederates. The poll was only about fifty percent and in some counties considerably less than that. The Republicans won handsomely with sixty-three counties against nineteen, and their victory could not be attributed to the black vote. In twenty-two Republican counties, the black population was negligible; in fourteen others, the blacks were in a small minority; and in only nine could the black vote have been decisive. This looked like a solid white Republican base in Tennessee, but there remained the awkward question of what would happen when the Confederate veterans recovered their votes. The answer was given in 1872 when the Democrats did much better in Tennessee than they did nationally; about 98,500 more votes were cast, and 69,500 of them went to the Democrats.[34]

If the Republicans hoped for the birth of white Republicanism in the lower South, the election of 1868 gave them little comfort. Every county they carried in Georgia had either a black majority or a very large minority. In some, a few white votes may have turned the balance, but overall it looked as though Republicanism in Georgia was black. It was the same story in Alabama, where only three "white" counties went Republican, of which two were small and thinly populated and the third was the well-known Unionist county of Randolph. It was much the same story in Louisiana where every Republican parish had a black majority. In South Carolina, all the counties carried by the Republicans had large black majorities except two where the races were approximately equal. These facts did not mean that no whites voted Republican—and they may have been more numerous than was sometimes believed—but the failure of Republicanism in predominantly white counties indicated that the Democrats could claim to be the white man's party. The Democrats carried some South Carolina counties where there were very large black minorities, thus indicating white solidarity behind the Democratic ticket.

Republicans hoped for better things in the former slave states of the Union. Maryland had been won by the Constitutional Unionists in 1860 and by Lincoln in 1864. In 1868, Maryland was not affected by the Reconstruction Acts; blacks did not vote and the result was disastrous for the Republicans. The Democrats were successful in every county but one, and their statewide majority was more than two to one. In 1872, with the blacks enfranchised by the Fifteenth Amendment, the Republican vote increased by over 36,000, but this was not enough to win them the state. Even more disastrous for the Republicans was the result in Kentucky. In

---

[34] The valuable collection of essays edited by Richard O. Curry, *Radicalism, Racism and Party Realignment: The Border States during Reconstruction,* (Baltimore, 1969), provides much information and analysis of problems that have so often been overlooked by historians of Reconstruction.

1864, Lincoln had received only 26,786 against 63,301 in a low poll, so a poor Republican showing was likely in 1868 and proved to be even worse than expected. The total vote was up by 65,000 and of this increased number no less than 52,600 went to the Democrats and only 12,700 to the Republicans. The nineteen counties carried by the Republicans were, with two exceptions, thinly populated "white" counties in the mountainous districts. A healthier result for the Republicans came from West Virginia, where their popular vote was 28,951 against 20,248 and they carried forty-one counties against twelve. Another fair prospect was revealed for the Republicans in Missouri. There the Republicans showed real vigor and carried eighty-four counties against twenty-seven; but, apart from a few districts, Missouri belonged to the Midwest rather than to the South. Moreover, the poll was low; many who had fought for the Confederacy were disfranchised, and the margin was uncomfortably narrow in sixteen counties where the Republican majority looked vulnerable. The year 1872 would see a great turnover with Missouri running strongly against the national trend to return a convincing Democratic majority. The result was somewhat confused because Missouri was a center of the liberal Republican revolt, but the state remained firmly Democratic in subsequent elections.

To sum up, the election of 1868 revealed that the hope of a Republican alliance in the South between the races was uncertain. In North Carolina, it looked as though a portion of the old Whig tradition in the white counties might be transformed into Republicanism, and, in Tennessee, there was some hope that the Republicans of both races would hold on to their advantage. In Arkansas, it looked as though Jacksonian nationalists had been converted to Republicanism. In the lower South, it was clear that white Republicanism could not survive without a large number of black voters. Republicanism had collapsed in Maryland, and the old Whig strength in Kentucky had passed over almost entirely to the Democrats. Missouri offered some comfort, but not enough to reassure discerning Republican leaders.

The election of 1868 had other unpleasant lessons for the Republicans. After the triumph of 1866, with legislative achievements of unprecedented significance, and having nominated the most popular man in the country, they found themselves with an unpleasantly narrow margin of victory. The result was more perplexing because the Democrats seemed to have mismanaged their campaign, and their revival could not be attributed to the popularity of Horatio Seymour, who had made a bad record (in Republican eyes) as the wartime governor of New York, was not the first choice of his party, disagreed with the party line on currency, and was urged to withdraw halfway through the campaign. As James G. Blaine observed in his memoirs:

Considering the time of the election, considering the record and the achievements of the rival candidates, the Presidential election of 1868 must be regarded as the most remarkable and the most unaccountable in our political annals.[35]

The reasons were perhaps less difficult to diagnose than Blaine suggested. The Republicans had spent too much time on failing to convict Johnson and too little on other problems of policy. An experienced politician and editor wrote from Chicago in July that the Republicans were "greatly disgusted and apathetic in consequence of the failure of impeachment." There was "no enthusiasm or self-sacrificing feeling among the rank and file," while the Democrats were "hungry and anxious for office and spoil." He predicted that Congress would adjourn without touching the financial questions, and this would be taken "as a confession . . . that the Republicans have no financial policy except high interest, untaxed lands and gold for the bond-holder with double taxation and depreciated shinplasters for the people."[36] In New Hampshire, another Republican believed that taxation would be the major issue.[37] There is therefore some evidence that the Republicans were not losing momentum on account of their Reconstruction policy but because preoccupation with it had prevented them from developing coherent ideas on other perplexing issues.[38] In March 1866, Horace Greeley had declared magisterially that "the Republican party must ultimately dissolve and pass away, as all other parties have done or should do." He had added, "It will die when its work is done, and not till then." On the morrow of Grant's election, the revival of the Democratic party raised the awkward question whether that demise was not now imminent,

[35] Blaine. *Twenty Years*, II, p. 408.

[36] Elihu B. Washburne Papers, Library of Congress, Horace Medill to E. B. W., July 10, 1868.

[37] *Ibid*. J. P. Ela to E. B. W., February 29, 1868.

[38] There may be some significance in the fact that James A. Garfield fought his own campaign in the Ohio 19th District almost exclusively on economic issues and won by a very large majority (Theodore Smith, *Garfield*, I. p. 138). Reconstruction had dominated the elections of 1866, and in any country voters become bored by repeat performances.

as it became apparent that the Republican party had not succeeded in making itself national.

Republicans were disturbed by the evidence of Democratic revival in what they regarded as their own heartland, but there was no cause for panic. Grant had won 214 electoral votes when he needed only 148 for a majority. Of Seymour's eighty electoral votes, thirty-three came from his own state of New York with a Democratic majority of only 9,968 out of nearly 450,000, or less than two percent. In the old free states, Grant's popular majority was 551,613. The slave states which had remained in the Union yielded a Democratic majority of 50,058, but this was in an area where Lincoln had gathered very few votes in 1860, so it might be that the star of Republicanism was rising over the border. The Republicans had also done very well in the congressional elections; in an enlarged House, the Democrats had improved upon their wretched 1866 showing to move from forty-nine to sixty-three; but the Republicans also added six seats and in the Senate their majority actually increased from thirty-one to forty-five.

On this showing, a Republican President could still win a future election without a vote in the South, and the party was assured of a two-thirds majority until March 1871. However, the party leaders wanted more than this. The Republican party must become national. The leaders had refused an opportunity of reconstructing the old Whig party within a Republican framework and had opted for a broad-based national alliance which would unite the middle-class liberalism of the North with the cause of the oppressed of both races in the South. Events would prove this to be a false dream, but one cannot understand the politics of Reconstruction without reckoning its influence upon Republican thinking.

The passage of the Fifteenth Amendment has been explained by the need for black votes in the marginal states of the North and Midwest. In Ohio, the Republican majority was a bare 0.8 percent of the votes cast; in Indiana, it was 2.76 percent. Illinois was healthier in Republican eyes, with a majority of 11.6 percent, but, in Pennsylvania, the majority was a little shaky at 4.4 percent. In Connecticut, it was a fraction over 3 percent. Those four states accounted for sixty-six electoral votes in 1868; and without them Grant would have had the bare majority necessary for election. The hypothesis that the primary purpose of the amendment was to save Republicanism in future elections in these marginal states has won widespread acceptance,[39] but it cannot be accepted as proven. The 1860 census showed 36,673 blacks in Ohio out of a population of 2,339,511; 11,428 out of 1,350,428 in Indiana; 56,849 out of 2,849,266 in Pennsylvania; and 8,627 out of 451,520 in Connecticut. The number of potential voters out of this total of 113,577 blacks in the marginal states would be about 22,700. The figures would have been a little larger by 1868, but the proportions remained the same, and there seems an inherent improbability in the suggestion that men would set out to amend the Constitution in order to secure an addition of about 1.6 percent to the total vote, even though they might hope to win it all for themselves.

The improbability increases when one looks at the situation in detail. In Ohio in 1860, there were twenty-six counties with a black population of over 500, and of these only two changed their party allegiance between 1868 and 1872. Hamilton, containing the city of Cincinnati and the largest black population, was carried for the Republicans by 5,600 in 1868 and by the Democrats by nearly 5,000 in 1872. One small county was carried for the Democrats by thirty in 1868, recaptured by the Republicans in 1872 and again by the Democrats in 1876. Four counties with significant black populations were carried by the Democrats in 1868 and retained by them after the passage of the Fifteenth Amendment. The only county in which black suffrage may have affected the result was Muskingum with a population of 43,326 in 1860, including 1,090 blacks in 1860. The Republicans won in 1868 by 150; in 1872, they won by 250; they lost by 200 in 1876; and they held it by very narrow majorities in 1880, 1884, and 1888. In such a marginal county, the 200 to 300 black voters were probably significant, but the results were so close that no one in 1869 could have foreseen the outcome. There were three other counties in which the retention of a small Republican majority may have been due to the black vote, but in a rapidly changing society, with so many variables affecting political behavior, it is difficult to form

---

[39] The view presented differs from that of William Gillette in *The Right to Vote: Politics and the Passage of the Fifteenth Amendment* (Baltimore, 1965). His view is accepted by David Donald who writes that Gillette "proves that its main purpose and its primary result was not to enfranchise black voters in the South . . . but in the North" (A. M. Schlesinger, ed., *History of U.S. Political Parties*, New York, 1973. II. 1290). If the election of 1868 was so close it was, however, of more importance to secure the black vote in the South against possible repeal of the Reconstruction Acts by a Democratic Congress, and of immediate importance to preserve black suffrage in Tennessee where it depended upon state law alone.

any firm conclusions. What does seem certain is that no one in 1869 could have calculated the consequences of black suffrage in Ohio, although it was natural for Republicans to stress its advantages to cautious colleagues who feared a mass desertion of whites from the party.

In Indiana, there were five or six thousand black voters after the Fifteenth Amendment, and these were worth having in a state where parties were evenly balanced. They were, however, widely dispersed and consequently their influence was diffused. No county had as many as 1,000 black inhabitants. Marion County, with 39,855 people in 1860 and the city of Indianapolis, had only 825 blacks. Clark County, across the river from Louisville, had only 520 out of 20,502. It is not therefore surprising that little effect of black voting can be detected in the county returns; indeed, there is perhaps a slight hint of white backlash in three counties carried for the Republicans by very small majorities in 1868 and captured by the Democrats in 1876. In Illinois, there were 7,628 blacks out of 1,711,951 in 1860; as in Indiana, they were widely dispersed and even Cook County, with a total population of 144,954, had only 1,007.

In Pennsylvania, three counties with significant black minorities were carried by the Democrats in 1868 and by the Republicans in 1872; but in each case, Democratic abstentions provided the answer, and all three returned to the Democrats in subsequent elections. The black vote may have helped to hold the marginal Franklin and Washington counties for the Republicans, and there they may have had an immediate incentive to support black suffrage; but in a state such as Pennsylvania, with growing industries and increasing numbers of immigrants, there were many other ethnic and emotional factors affecting party allegiance.

The situation in the northern and midwestern states provided no compelling reason for Republican leaders to press on with the Fifteenth Amendment. The possible gains were too narrow to calculate with exactness; the risks of white reaction and the consequences of failure to ratify were too great. Common sense suggests that, in pressing the amendment, the Republicans were seeking to broaden and strengthen the national base of their party and were not preoccupied by the problem of a few marginal constituencies.

Some Republicans had been convinced since the Emancipation of the need for Negro suffrage; some had come to accept it as a measure of justice; while others saw it mainly as an instrument to counter the resurgent authority of the southern upper class. The mixture of idealism and partisan calculation is familiar, and one can hardly achieve results without the other. The purpose of the present argument is not to examine the idealism which inspired some in the quest for equality but to examine the political calculations which may have entered into the attempt to nationalize the Republican party. In 1869, the heart of the problem was still the South and the hope was to establish a party organization in all states of the Union. Experienced national politicians knew this would serve their party even if it was doomed to be a minority in some states for many years to come. An organization acted as a nucleus to attract the discontented or to exploit divisions among the majority, and, without a party in being, others would benefit from these events. The Republicans were desperately anxious to establish white party organizations in the South, but their base was still insecure. The election of 1868 presented some encouraging features, but it had not seen southern Unionists emerge in large numbers, take charge of the situation, and join with their natural allies in the Republican party.

In the lower South, it therefore became of crucial importance to preserve Republicanism by securing the black vote. It still depended upon an act of Congress (which could be repealed), and, once the states had been readmitted to the Union, little could be done to stop them from disenfranchising the blacks. The Fourteenth Amendment had, it is true, imposed a penalty for denying the vote to any substantial number of citizens, but this would be difficult and perhaps impossible to operate. Radicals saw therefore the need to remove suffrage from exclusive control by the states, embody it in the Constitution beyond the reach of simple majorities in Congress, and protect the right to vote by national authority. They would have preferred a positive requirement for universal male suffrage, and a straightforward assertion of federal responsibility for it. They had to be content with a prohibition which left the initiative to the states and implicitly gave Congress the right to intervene only when infringement was proved. Nevertheless, this was better than nothing, and, almost as soon as it had been ratified, the Republican majority passed an enforcement act.

In ten states of the former Confederacy, the rationale of the Fifteenth Amendment depended upon hypothetical calculations of what would happen to the black vote and the Republican party if Congress no longer had the power to control the situation by law. In the border states, the case for the amendment was urgent and directly related to the immediate prospects of the Republican party. The Reconstruction Acts did not apply to Tennessee, because the state had quickly ratified the Fourteenth Amendment and thereby earned readmission. Under William G. Brownlow, the Unionists had seized control, imposed drastic disenfranchisement upon all who had actively helped the Confederacy, and given the vote to the blacks. But all this depended upon state law, and there was doubt about how long the structure of radical Unionism could resist pressure. In Delaware, Maryland, Kentucky, and Missouri, there was no black suffrage, and Unionism was in danger as the Confederates came home.

In Tennessee as in North Carolina, there was indeed a large nucleus for indigenous white Republicanism. Thirteen "white" counties, which had been Whig in the past, would be consistently Republican in the postwar years; seven former "white" Whig counties switched to the Democrats, but this was offset by eight white counties which had been Democrat in 1852 and became firmly Republican after 1865. Of the seventy-nine counties in the state, there were therefore twenty-one, mainly in eastern Tennessee, which became consistently Republican. In addition, there were eighteen former white Democratic counties which went Republican in 1868, but the polls were very low and Republican success depended upon the disenfranchisement of their opponents; but even if they lost at subsequent elections, their Republican organization would remain in fighting trim. However, with twenty-one counties more or less certain and eighteen more in which they might stand a chance of success, the Republicans might still be short of a majority (on a full white vote); this made the ten counties with black majorities and the seven others with large black minorities crucial for the future of the party in the state. The need for a constitutional amendment guaranteeing black suffrage before the Democrats recaptured a majority of the white vote was clear.

Kentucky was a lost cause for Republicanism in 1868, but there were enough Unionists to make it worthwhile to bolster their organization in the hope of winning state and congressional elections. The Republicans in the state certainly preferred to have black suffrage forced upon them by federal action than to incur the odium of fighting for it as a local issue. Some had already asked for the state to be reconstructed by Congress, because the Confederates had returned in such numbers and, unlike Tennessee, suffered no penalties or disqualifications. The black vote could not upset the Democratic ascendancy, but it might strengthen the opposition and provide a Republican base for future operations.

In Maryland, the black vote could be crucial. Without it, the Democrats had swept the board in 1868, but hard-pressed Republicans could see some hope in the sixteen counties (out of twenty-one) which the Democrats had carried by narrow margins. In addition, there were 5,700 potential voters in Baltimore; this would not overcome the 1868 Democratic majority of 12,500 but would narrow the gap and have some effect in municipal elections. Maryland radicals were bolder than those of Kentucky on the question of suffrage, but they too welcomed the prospect of federal action rather than a state campaign which would generate bitterness without prospect of success. In 1872, the suffrage gamble seemed to have paid off handsomely. All but one of the marginal counties went Republican, and the Democratic majority in Baltimore was cut to just over 5,000, although this was just enough to win the state by less than 1,000. This success was, however, partly the consequence of Democratic disarray; in subsequent years, the Democrats rallied, enacted ingenious registration laws to keep many blacks from the polls, and won in 1876 with a majority of over 20,000 in the state. However, this was narrowed to just over 15,000 in 1880 and 11,000 in 1884. Black suffrage had not given the state to the Republicans, but, in spite of devices to keep them from voting, they continued to do so in large numbers, and the Republican party remained as a respectable minority and a vigorous opposition. Thus the Fifteenth Amendment preserved the two-party system in Maryland.

Nowhere did the Republicans hope for better results from the amendment than in Missouri. In 1860, the white population was 1,063,509; there were 114,931 slaves and 3,572 free blacks. In thirty-nine counties out of 112, the black population exceeded 500, and, in nineteen of them, it was over 1,500. This would not in itself have made the foundation for a party, but, combined with vigorous white Unionism, it might be very significant. The sweeping Republican victories of 1868 had been won without the black vote but with disenfranchisement of former Confederates. The potential 20,000 black votes were therefore of considerable importance and might have had more permanent consequences if it had not been for the liberal Republican revolt of 1872. This took many Unionists into fusion with the Democrats, and few returned to the Republican party. The thirty or so counties which settled permanently in the Republican column were all "white" counties, and all those with 1,500 or more blacks became permanently Democratic. In only three counties was the margin close enough and the black vote large enough to play a significant part in Republican success. Nevertheless, in Missouri as in Maryland, the Fifteenth Amendment helped if it did not cause the survival of a two-party system.

In two other border states—Delaware and West Virginia—the black vote was too small to have any significant effect. There was, however, one great Confederate state where the issue had yet to be tried. Virginia had been excluded in 1868, so there was no evidence as yet of its behavior in a national election. The Republicans could hardly hope to conquer at one blow the great citadel of the Confederacy, yet there were signs which encouraged them to hope. There were certainly Unionists in Virginia; some of them had supported the shadow Union government during the war, and Governor Pierpont had been well received when he took over in 1865 as the chief official of the state. There were a large number of western counties with long traditions of hostility to rule by the planter-gentry and the merchants of Richmond. On the other hand, there were also many planters and merchants, anxious to establish stable relations with the North, who might look with favor upon the old Whig element in the Republican party. Finally, there were a large number of counties with black majorities and an almost equally large number with very large black minorities. A rough calculation gives forty-six "white" counties, twenty-nine with large white majorities, thirty-three with smaller white majorities, and thirty-nine with black majorities. Black suffrage was, of course, already the law under the Reconstruction Act, but the Republican stake was so large that it was an additional argument (if one were needed) for a federal amendment to preserve it. If white Unionism could be persuaded to amalgamate with black Republicanism, the party would have the promise of a healthy life in all the upper South, from Missouri in the west to Virginia and North Carolina in the east.

The political history of Virginia is therefore a comment upon the failure of Republican hopes for nationalizing their party. Twenty-eight counties became permanently Republican, and thirteen others were marginal but leaned to the Republicans; of these forty-two counties, only one was "white," and only three had large white majorities; seven contained large black minorities; and thirty-one had black majorities. Republicanism staggered on in the late nineteenth century, but in only four counties was it the majority party of the white men; in seven, it survived in alliance with the blacks; and, in thirty-one, it depended upon a black majority. Most former Whigs and Unionists found their way into the dominant Democratic party. This was symptomatic of the Republican failure to build a truly national and biracial party and indicative of the wider failure to reconstruct a national two-party system. There can be little doubt that this failure was a tragedy for the United States and for the South, and it is therefore worthwhile to conclude this essay with a few speculations about its causes.[40] These are to be sought in the character of southern society, the plight of the upper class, and a grim struggle for power between old leaders and new claimants.

The most obvious characteristic of the South had been slavery, but intense discussion of this topic has often diverted attention away from the class structure of southern white society. The men who ruled the South were drawn very largely from the class of wealthy planters, together with their lawyer allies and a small number of men who made a career in public life. The lawyers and the political careerists usually acquired land and slaves so that their style of life came to resemble that of the planters. The same is true of the small number of merchants and professional men who acquired influence in their communities. The upper class was not a caste, and it was comparatively easy for a man of talents or acquired wealth to enter it; but it was definitely class-conscious, and its members were set off from all other men by their style and the conventions they observed. The upper class monopolized public office at the state level and controlled those counties dominated by the plantation culture, and, in spite of criticism voiced by spokesmen of the rural middle class, the planter-gentry had learned how to maintain their ascendancy in a democratic society. At any time, the white majority could have wrecked the power of the upper class by normal political action; they did not do so, and those of their representatives who rose to power and authority were quickly assimilated into the ruling class.

Before 1850, the southern upper class had been divided politi-

[40] For Virginia during Reconstruction see the valuable monograph by Jack P. Maddex, Jr., *The Virginia Conservatives, 1867-1879* (Chapel Hill, N.C., 1970). In Virginia, the Reconstruction story was somewhat different from that of other states, and in a sense Virginia was never "reconstructed." The Unionist government of Francis Pierpont took over quietly after the fall of the Confederacy, but the Unionist government was quickly dominated by conservatives. Though temporarily disorganized by the Reconstruction Acts, the radical threat forced the conservatives together and into cooperation with the Democratic party, and they won the first state election held under the Reconstruction Acts.

cally between a Whig majority and a Democratic minority, but, in the years preceding the Civil War, these distinctions became blurred as men of both parties turned to the common task of defending their section, their class, and the economic base of their power. Yet every southern gentleman who defended slavery was also aware that the men who could deprive him of office and influence were not in the North but amongst the plain people for whom he claimed to speak. This was the only alternative power in the South, and it could be summoned from the depths by the simple act of casting votes. The essential character of this class rule had not been changed by the war, but, for the moment, it looked as though the war had undermined the structure of political power. In this view, the crucial issue during Reconstruction was not the attempt of northern radicals to impose their system but the sustained effort of the southern upper class to maintain their position.

The upper class had been gravely weakened by the war. In many cases, their accumulated wealth had evaporated, and their property had been partly destroyed. The end of slavery, coming on top of inflation, meant the disappearance of a huge capital investment. Their prestige as leaders had suffered, for individual heroism could not entirely obscure the long story of blunder and miscalculation. They knew, too, that in the North every encouragement would be given to their rivals; yet it was the paradox of their situation that recovery could not be accomplished without northern aid. A principal stake in the southern power struggle was therefore the goodwill of northern business and access to northern capital; this prize was likely to be won by those who could demonstrate their political control of the southern states.[41]

The upper class had altered in subtle but important ways as a consequence of the war. Natural selection had been at work to eliminate the least efficient, and those who survived were forced by circumstances to diversify their efforts. The men who took the economic lead in the postwar South were resilient, resourceful, and determined in their quest for economic gain. Ruin was the alternative, and they could not afford to relax their efforts. The southern upper class was therefore transformed by war into something much more like modern capitalists than the prewar

[41] For a detailed study of southern reactions see Michael Perman, *Reunion without Compromise: The South and Reconstruction, 1865-1868* (Cambridge, England, 1973). My own emphasis is somewhat different from Mr. Perman's, but his account of the political tactics of southern leaders is convincing.

planter-gentry. At the same time, they confronted, for the first time, new rivals in both the economic and political spheres. Entrepreneurs, men eager to buy land, and speculators came south in large numbers; they constituted a threat to the upper class which might be difficult to contain, because they already enjoyed or could readily obtain goodwill and material assistance from the North. In other parts of the Union, the arrival of hopeful and ambitious men from outside was so normal an occurrence that it passed either without notice or with a few formal words of welcome. In the South, they represented a new and unfamiliar threat to the order already shaken by war.

Thus the aspirations of the upper class were threatened on two fronts by the southern white majority and by newcomers from the North. If the political and economic forces of their rivals were allied, the upper class would be forced to retreat, surrender its monopoly of political power, and make what terms they could for a share of economic power. This was the principal feature of the grim struggle for power which developed in the South, as the upper class, chastened and purged by war, sought to defend its economic and political status.

The conventions which met in 1865 under the Johnson plan were crucial. They have received little detailed study, but what there has been suggests that the majority of delegates were lawyers, farmers, some small planters, and a few merchants.[42] The President's exemptions from amnesty included not only all high civil officials and military officers but also all active supporters of the Confederacy with property valued at more than $20,000. Here then was the opportunity for new leaders to take charge, but in most cases it seems that the few experienced members of the old upper class were able to dominate the proceedings. Perhaps in the circumstances of 1865, no one else had the heart or interest to take the initiative. Even more striking was the way in which the old upper class reasserted itself in the elections that followed, and dozens of men still exempted from amnesty were chosen for state offices. The large number of prominent ex-Confederates chosen as representatives designate for Congress quickly became notorious in the

[42] Alan Conway, *The Reconstruction of Georgia* (Minneapolis, 1966), pp. 44-45, quotes some conflicting contemporary comments on the social composition and quality of the 1865 convention. The comments which stress the previous insignificance and lack of social distinction of the delegates seem most convincing; perhaps for this reason the convention was quickly dominated by Herschel V. Johnson and Charles J. Jenkins, who had both been prominent lawyers before the war. All comments agreed upon the conservative character of the convention.

North. President Johnson found himself in a cruel dilemma; he had hoped to instigate a democratic revolution and now found representatives of the upper class (which he had spent his life in opposing) elected to office by democratic procedures which he himself had laid down. Moreover, it seemed likely that local government would not function at all if he began a purge of officials still excluded from amnesty. There was no alternative but to legalize the voters' choice by issuing pardons. It is also probable that Johnson was influenced by the argument that so long as the titles to so much landed property remained in doubt (because the owners were unpardoned) it would be difficult to impose order upon the troubled southern society.

Within a few months of disastrous defeat, the prospect for the southern upper class had suddenly improved. There was still a long way to go for economic recovery, but political ascendancy had been restored. The black codes imposed discipline upon the black labor, guaranteed the poorer whites against the black incursion into traditionally white districts, and severely restricted a black descent upon the towns. Given this framework of law, most former slaveowners found it surprisingly easy to adapt to abolition. It is true that there were many examples of plantation owners who could not or would not understand how to operate wage labor, but the men at the head of affairs quickly realized that if free labor had to be paid it could also be fired and that the employer incurred no responsibility for the young, sick, or aged. Black civil rights were no great threat; indeed, there might be advantages in being able to sue blacks or call black witnesses. The Freedmen's Bureau might cause some friction if the officers were overzealous, but a good many of them understood that their job was to get the freedmen to work, and, in the dislocated state of society, it was useful to have someone to hear complaints and distribute relief. In the early part of 1866, the men in charge of the new state governments could therefore regard with some equanimity the determination of Congress to protect Negro rights, although they resented the continued exclusion of their representatives from Congress.

The disqualification clause of the Fourteenth Amendment presented a threat of an entirely different order. If it became effective, the whole structure of power created during the preceding twelve months would collapse. Acceptance of the amendment would mean voluntary abdication, and, by the time that Congress saw fit to remove the disabilities, new men would have established themselves politically and earned the confidence of northern capitalists. Faced with this prospect, rejection of the amendment was the only answer; the reactions of Congress were foreseen— though the Reconstruction Acts may have been more drastic than they expected—but southern leaders knew that their position would be stronger if they were forced out by Congress rather than if they meekly consented to their own elimination. There was a risk, but it seemed worth taking, and events would justify the decision.[43]

Under the Reconstruction Acts, the real danger came not from Negro suffrage in itself but from the possibility that the new political system would open the door for vigorous, ambitious men to fill the void in leadership. Moreover, there was the additional danger, as the new leaders established themselves, that enough white southerners would be attracted by the bait of economic advantage to join them. Here was a new element in the situation, and for the moment the southern upper class looked to the future with divided counsels. Some advised cooperation, some resistance; the preservation of upper class leadership remained the ultimate objective, but there was some fumbling over means. The exploitation of anti-Negro terrorism was an error when it led to violence, because this, more than anything else, was likely to forfeit the goodwill of northern businessmen and throw their support behind the radical governments. Far better results were achieved by a campaign of propaganda which raised the bogey of Negro rule for home consumption, and of corruption, inefficiency, and waste to enlighten northern business. In the event, the Negro was inevitably a casualty in this struggle for power, but Negro rule was never a possibility, and the vital question of Reconstruction had always been which whites should rule.

This analysis may suggest too great a rationality on the part of men who had always had political instincts rather than political ideas. The truth is that Reconstruction politics in the South grew out of prewar politics, and the upper class did not have to invent but merely to adapt. The unusual combination of class rule with wide suffrage had always existed, and southern leaders had always lived with the problem of preserving power when the electoral cards seemed to be stacked against them. But in applying familiar modes of behavior, they also presented a classic example of the

---

[43] For arguments in the South over the Fourteenth Amendment see Michael Perman, *Reunion without Compromise*, Ch. 8.

way in which a capitalist class could ward off social revolution and survive intact in a democratic society.[44] The true measure of their success was the defeat which they inflicted upon Republicanism despite its command of all the resources of middle class liberalism. In time of test, the system of values embodied in this ideology could not stand up to the power of dynamic capitalism. For good or ill, this is perhaps the way it always will be.

Although the failure to restore a national two-party system must therefore be understood primarily with reference to the structure of southern society, this is not quite the last word. If the Republicans wanted to win southern white support, it was up to them to raise the stake. The collapse of Republicanism in the South is normally explained by southern resistance to black suffrage and office holding, but prejudice, though strong, is not immune to other pressures. If the Republicans had been able to offer stronger inducements to southern white farmers and to the small number of wealthy men who joined their party, the outcome might have been different. The Republicans, bound by the social philosophy of the age, could not do much to promote directly the economic advancement of depressed and backward areas. Everything that the Republicans spoke about in their customary rhetoric—industry, railroads, education, and opportunity—had to come from private enterprise or state governments. A Tennessee Valley Authority was beyond the range of political possibility or social imagination. Congress even rejected a well-conceived plan for a national education scheme which would have benefited the illiterate of both races. Eventually, the rise of the southern textile industry did more to put money into the pockets of the poorer whites than all the laws of Congress. Republicanism could represent well enough the aspirations of expanding northern and western societies, but it could not imagine the scale of aid necessary for an underdeveloped region. When Republicanism had so little positive inducement to offer, it is no surprise that class and race came to dominate the politics of a one-party South.

[44] The nature of the conflict in one state was diagnosed with great ability many years ago by Roger W. Shugg in *Origins of the Class Struggle in Louisana* (Baton Rouge, 1939; second printing 1966).

OTTO H. OLSEN

Southern Reconstruction and the Question of Self-Determination

Historical revision is common to every generation, but certainly ours has revised the history of southern Reconstruction with more than common vigor. Reconstruction historians of today repudiate most earlier authorities as impossibly racist; they applaud long-disgraced southern Republicans; and they denounce once-honored redeemers. Cherished stereotypes have fallen as that entire group of formerly infamous scoundrels—carpetbaggers, scalawags, and freed blacks—have been accorded new appreciation and respect. An era once equated with depravity and evil has become identified with enlightenment and reform, and the tragedy of Reconstruction in the South has become its failure rather than its fact.

Above all else this changing consensus respecting the Reconstruction South reflects the racial and political equalitarianism of the present day, and no quarrel is raised here with an overdue correction of the white supremacist nonsense of the past. It is appropriate, however, to caution our new enthusiasm against either romanticizing Reconstruction or exaggerating the independent role of white racism in that experience. Furthermore, despite the growing chorus of Reconstruction applause, historians remain perplexed by the fact of Reconstruction failure, and it begs the question of explaining that failure to suggest that a more radical

113

though unattainable program might have brought more success. In response to such considerations, this essay is intended to summarize recent interpretive trends while also qualifying them, especially by reconsidering the importance of old but neglected questions of alien domination and home rule.

We must not leave our beautiful country to the vilest of tories and to the vilest of our enemies.

> Daniel H. Hill
> Former Confederate General
> December 28, 1866

These governments are in external form civil, but they are in their essential principle military. They are called local governments, but in reality they are Federal executive agencies. . . . They are as completely insulated from the traditions, the feelings, the interests, and the free suffrages of the people, white and black, as if they were outside the limits of those States.

> Lucius Q. C. Lamar
> Mississippi Congressman
> June 8, 1874

The Republican party was never indigenous to Southern soil. In truth, it has never become acclimated there, but has remained from the first an exotic.

> Albion W. Tourgee
> Carpetbagger, 1878

The basic political problem facing the reunited states in 1865 was how to determine satisfactorily the permanent results of a civil war that was unusually sectional in nature. Four years of brutal fighting left a legacy hindering easy reconciliation, while drastic changes wrought by war presented various enduring demands. Most obviously the southern attempt at independence had served to accelerate precisely those revolutionary developments that the South so greatly feared—the freeing of and extension of rights to former black slaves, the verification and expansion of federal supremacy, and an increase in the power of industrial and commercial forces in American life. The precise extent or meaning of such changes, however, was not apparent at the conclusion of the war, and subsequent efforts to define these changes were greatly complicated by the continuing vitality of the recently Confederate South.

It was northern Republicans who claimed the fruits of victory, and, though tainted by self-righteousness and desires for vengeance, Republican concerns were generally pertinent and reasonable ones. Above all, they wanted assurances of the continuing permanence of the Union and the full achievement of emancipation. They demanded an extension of rights and privileges to blacks consistent with their state of freedom, and they expected that the South would concede a new dignity and prominence to southern whites who had remained loyal to the Union. Republicans were divided in their approach to these matters, but they were united in seeing themselves as entitled to enforce the terms of an essentially unconditional military victory. They were not prepared immediately to allow vanquished but still suspect traitors to participate as equals in defining those terms.

But the North, let alone the Republican party, was not synonymous with the entire nation, and, as lasting disagreements arose over the terms of peace, the question also arose of how far the North was entitled to go in retaining sole control of the federal government and forcing conditions upon the South that had not been clearly defined by the war's end. A resultant postwar dilemma reflected the sectional nature of the war and the federalist structure of the nation, and this dilemma was intensified by two years of wrangling delay occasioned by both northern vacillation and the premature boldness of the defeated South. Contributing immensely to this delay was Abraham Lincoln's assassination and the elevation to the Presidency of a southern Democrat, Andrew Johnson from Tennessee. Although Johnson was a staunch opponent of the Confederacy, he disrupted the Reconstruction process by his stubborn attempt to effect a rapid restoration of the Union without fully satisfying the expectations of the victorious North.

Since Congress was not in session when Johnson assumed the Presidency in April 1865, he was free to initiate a plan of his own which promised to restore the southern states to an equal place in the Union upon their organization of new state governments committed to a formal endorsement of emancipation and a repudiation of both secession and the Confederate war debt. During May, the President instituted restoration procedures by recognizing four state governments established under federal auspices during the war and appointing provisional governors in the remaining states. Former rebels were pardoned upon taking a simple oath of allegiance, and, although fourteen classes of prominent southern leaders were excluded from this pardon, including all citizens possessing property assessed at $20,000 or more, special pardons were extended rather freely to the exempted groups.

Initially, the presidential program promised well. All of the provisional governors had opposed secession; five of the seven were associated with opposition to the southern war effort; and only one had been prominent in the Confederacy.[1] Much the same was true of the convention delegates elected to institute the restoration procedures. The President's demands were then met, although not always gracefully, and northern Republicans awaited further reassuring signs from the South. Instead, southern leaders displayed a disturbingly aggressive attitude that had been preluded by their strong objections to the dissolution of Confederate state authority at the end of the war.[2] Undoubtedly encouraged by the lenient presidential program, the traditional leaders of the South, most of whom were closely identified with slavery and the Confederacy, now asserted themselves with such vigor as to arouse northern fears and undermine the presidential program itself.

The strength and persistence of this disruptive southern behavior was rooted in national tradition and cultural fact. The size and federalist structure of the United States had always encouraged diversity and local allegiance, and nowhere was a contrast more apparent than between the slave states and the free. According to the dominant southern point of view, a citizen's primary allegiance rested with the state, and a state did have the right to secede. Thus, despite extensive opposition to the policy of secession in the prewar South, once a state did secede, its white population and leadership could and did unite firmly in support of the Confederacy and its subsequent war against a foreign aggressor. The subsequent War between the States or War for Southern Independence, as it was perceived by the South, largely solidified state and sectional rather than national loyalties in both North and South, and these loyalties were not obliterated by either victory or defeat. This is not to deny that the Confederacy was greatly troubled by persistent Unionism and a growing disillusionment

---

[1] The anti-Confederate record of the provisional governors appears understated in Michael Perman, *Reunion without Compromise: The South and Reconstruction, 1865-1868* (Cambridge, 1973). Cf. Walter L. Fleming, *Civil War and Reconstruction in Alabama* (New York, 1905), p. 143; C. Mildred Thompson, *Reconstruction in Georgia: Economic, Social, Political, 1865-1872* (New York, 1915), p. 145; William C. Harris, *Presidential Reconstruction in Mississippi* (Baton Rouge, 1967), pp. 12, 41.

[2] When the Mississippi legislature was ordered dissolved and Confederate Governor Charles Clarke arrested by the federal commander, he objected: "I am the duly and constitutionally elected governor of the state of Mississippi, and would resist, if in my power, to the last extremity the enforcement of your order." James W. Garner, *Reconstruction in Mississippi* (New York, 1901), p. 60, n. 3.

with the war. There is, however, little to indicate that widespread defeatism during the latter years of the war promoted either love of the Union (which in postwar parlance was too often synonymous with the North) or an intrinsic opposition to the idea of state or sectional autonomy.[3]

It was especially obvious that the leadership of the South lamented the Confederacy's defeat. "The people who felt most bitterly at the end of the war," said one of them, "were not the majority in numbers but they were the majority so to speak in social rank and influence, refinement, intelligence and wealth."[4] Although momentarily subdued, these proud leaders were neither silent nor inactive in behalf of their own interests. Having already suffered defeat, humiliation, and tremendous financial losses, they were additionally exasperated by the domineering position of a self-righteous North and by a variety of challenges from freed slaves and anti-Confederate political opponents. Anxious to restore the prosperity and stability of a devastated land, they were also quick to resent and resist any further erosion of their own wealth and power from either internal or external sources.

Probably the greatest problem facing the South was that of recovering from the havoc of war. An astounding proportion of the region's white manhood had been crippled or killed, and the destruction of property and livestock in much of the South was immense. Vast amounts of accumulated wealth had been lost or destroyed by emancipation, repudiation, general bankruptcy, tax sales, and foreclosures. Agriculture, manufacturing, and transportation had been widely disrupted. Where now was capital and leadership to be obtained for revival and restoration? How were race relations to be dealt with, and how was free black labor to be effectively organized and controlled?

As the white leaders of the South undertook the difficult tasks of establishing order, restoring production, and generally recovering from the war, they resented interference from an obviously distrustful and unsympathetic North. They were particularly annoyed by northern meddling in southern race and labor relation-

---

[3] Satisfactory accounts of all or portions of the history of the Reconstruction South as a whole are rare, and the conclusions in this essay are based primarily upon state and biographical studies. Though marred by racism and hostility to Republicanism, the works of the Dunning school in many ways remain invaluable, as do the works of older black and radical historians and more recent revisionists. A thorough documentation of the generalizations presented in this essay is impractical, and documentation will remain very selective.

[4] Cornelia P. Spencer, "A Sketch of the University of North Carolina," C. P. Spencer Papers, Southern Historical Collection, University of North Carolina.

ships, and they believed that northern charity was excessively
concerned with the problems of blacks while neglecting those of
whites. Ignoring their own responsibility for the plight of the
South, these southern leaders also privately and publicly denounced the North for its military devastation and destruction of
slavery, its collection of new cotton and old land taxes, its talk of
punishment and confiscation, and any and all of its continuing
interference in southern affairs.

To a significant degree, southern whites were renewing a
struggle recently waged not only against the North but also
frequently against the central authority of the Confederacy itself—a struggle against any external domination. Federalist and
states' rights principles formed a crucial part of this rationale, but
southern attitudes also reflected ages of sectional distinction and
conflict that had established a lasting sense of separate identity
and hostility toward the North. White southerners who accepted
defeat and reunion, and even emancipation, as the legitimate
results of the war continued to maintain a strong, even primary,
allegiance to their state, their section, and their "lost cause" that
can only be described as quasi-national in nature and intensity.
They spoke repeatedly of "our country," our "beloved South,"
and our "poor Southland" and often compared their fate with
that of the Irish, the Poles, or the Swiss.[5]

The fact was that issues of cultural clash and self-determination
were entwined in Reconstruction that could not and cannot be
resolved simply by glorifying the northern cause and insisting that
the United States was one indivisible nation. The South had been
kept in the Union only by force; it remained dominated by whites
who had been committed to slavery and the Confederacy; and it
was capable of resisting interference in its internal affairs whether
directly by the federal government or indirectly through the
encouragement of minority reformist and anti-Confederate factions
within the South.

While significant political transitions reflecting the outcome of
the war were under way in the postwar South, these constituted
little concession to the North, although they did involve a
confusing conception of "Unionism" that catered to southern
rather than northern concerns. This peculiar brand of southern

[5] A. M. McPheeters to Rufus L. Patterson, June 10, 1865, Patterson Papers, North
Carolina State Archives; Laura Mordecai to Marcus L. Ward, February 4, 1866, Pattie
Mordecai Collection, North Carolina State Archives; Drury Lacy to C. P. Spencer,
November 11, 1865, David Lowry Swain Papers, Southern Historical Collection,
University of North Carolina.

"Unionism" exploited disillusionment with the war by blaming both the initiation and the failure of that war upon original secessionists, Democrats, and supporters of the Confederate administration of Jefferson Davis. Even before the war ended, those groups were frequently displaced from state power by a Conservative party composed of antebellum Unionists and Whigs who had been among the last to endorse secession. Southern Conservatives were thus Confederates, often ardent and prominent ones, who denied any significant responsibility for the existence of the Civil War. After the war ended, this claim of the Conservatives was offered as a justification for restoring them to power while denying the aspirations of consistent wartime Unionists or peace advocates, both of whom were generally condemned as traitors by the dominant white South. The North was not receptive to these developments. Conservatives could not this easily excuse their Confederate record, and they remained annoyingly immoderate in their attitude toward the North. Considering abolitionists and Republicans even more responsible for the war than secessionists, the Conservative-Confederates lacked a cooperative attitude toward northern Republicans, and their political success was often at the expense of southern leaders who advised catering more fully to the demands of the victors.[6]

Blaming a disastrous and unpopular war on radicals in both sections of the nation, Conservative-Confederates insisted that they necessarily had gone with their state after all feasible alternatives had been destroyed. They were proud of having served the Confederacy honorably and well. Now they accepted defeat, emancipation, and reunion and felt entitled to an immediate restoration of an antebellum condition which they had never wished to disrupt. They accused the Republicans of perpetuating disunion and denying the southern states their existing constitutional rights, which included a voice in determining all subsequent federal policy.[7] Encouraged in their stance by the northern Democratic party, by President Johnson, and by their own

[6] Alan Conway, *The Reconstruction of Georgia* (Minneapolis, 1966), pp. 51-52; Harris, *Presidential Reconstruction in Mississippi*, pp. 112-15; Otto H. Olsen, *Carpetbagger's Crusade: The Life of Albion W. Tourgee* (Baltimore, 1965), pp. 38-41.

[7] According to Alexander H. Stephens, Vice President of the Confederacy, southern whites "expected as soon as the confederate cause was abandoned that immediately the states would be brought back into their practical relations with the government as previously constituted." They believed that the only possible justification for the war against them was that they always had remained in the Union as equal states: Walter L. Fleming (ed.), *Documentary History of Reconstruction: Political, Military, Social, Religious, Educational, and Industrial, 1865 to the Present Time* (2 vols., Cleveland, 1906-1907), vol. I, p. 234.

misreading of northern sentiment, southern leaders clearly had
adopted an offensive rather than conciliatory strategy. Initially,
many were even critical of the presidential program, although as
the struggle between Johnson and the Republican Congress ma-
tured, the leaders of the South aligned themselves with the
President and thereafter felt little or no legal or moral obligation
to any Reconstruction demands beyond those initially imposed by
him. The Freedmen's Bureau, military intervention, and other
federal activities were all denounced, and there was no serious
consideration of suggestions that northern radicalism be out-
maneuvered by extending additional equality to a select minority
of blacks. It was the southern leadership's defiance of more
popular and moderate northern expectations, however, that paved
the way for a Reconstruction far more radical and disruptive than
the North itself intended. Indicative of a bold and mistaken
confidence, southern whites elected to the federal Congress of
1865 the former Vice President of the Confederacy, nine Confederate army officers, six Confederate cabinet officials, and fifty-
eight Confederate Congressmen.

Disturbed and exasperated by such boldness, Congress responded by denying admission to southern representatives. Meanwhile,
Republicans had become additionally upset by the reported
mistreatment of blacks and white Unionists in the South. Not only
were wartime Union men, whom the North considered steadfast
national patriots, unable to capture political power in the former
Confederate states, but it was soon apparent that they were a
despised and mistreated minority there. It was also obvious that,
despite a common white racism, there were substantial differences
between the northern and southern conceptions of emancipation.

As representatives of the military and a free enterprise system,
federal authorities in the postwar South were not overly senti-
mental toward a landless, laboring class, but their policies were
favorable to the blacks insofar as they were directed against certain
vestiges of racism and slavery. Southern whites, on the other hand,
were inclined by habit, racism, and self-interest toward customary
methods of controlling black labor that were all too reminiscent of
slavery. Generally speaking, southern Negroes were consigned to a
status of extreme inferiority, and force and cruel injustice were
freely used to keep them there. Negro education, landownership,
and entrepreneurship were resented, mocked, and often hindered.
Racial inequalities were established by laws varying in their
oppressiveness but   thoroughly outraging the North. A leading

scholar concluded of a Mississippi black code that "almost every act, word, or gesture not consonant with good taste and good manners, as well as good morals, was made a crime or misdemeanor, for which [a freedman] could be fined by the magistrate, and then consigned to a condition of almost slavery for an indefinite time, if he could not pay the fine."[8] Atrocities against blacks were also widespread and would be highlighted by racist massacres in New Orleans and Memphis during 1866. Although the more vicious racists admittedly were a minority of the whites, their actions were freely tolerated by the community at large.

This postwar oppression of southern blacks affected federal Reconstruction policy primarily by convincing many northerners that certain manifestations of slavery were being perpetuated in the South. But the condition and role of the freed black population was also central to the history of Reconstruction in other ways and deserves some additional examination.

The plight of oppressed blacks was intensified by a condition that is difficult to comprehend.[9] The former slaves were despised, penniless, and largely illiterate, without even a full name or a title to the rags on their backs. They were largely unaware of the demands and the ways of freedom, and they were granted little in the way of respect, rights, or power. Emancipation was hardly freedom at all, but only an end to slavery, only the beginning of a long, hard trek that began with little more than the freedom to claim a name or the right to marry and keep one's own children, the freedom to work for pay (though perhaps never receive it), and the right just to get up and go. This was the humble beginning of a self-directed life for one-third of the population of the South, and the very start and extent of black progress in the face of endless resistance, betrayal, and hardship was probably the greatest reconstruction of all.

The former slave population's awareness of freedom was hardly

---

[8] John W. Burgess, *Reconstruction and the Constitution*, 1866-1876 (New York, 1902), p. 53.

[9] The best accounts are Willie Lee Rose, *Rehearsal for Reconstruction: The Port Royal Experiment* (New York, 1964); Joel Williamson, *After Slavery: The Negro in South Carolina During Reconstruction, 1861-1877* (Chapel Hill, N.C., 1965) Joe M. Richardson, *The Negro in the Reconstruction of Florida, 1865-1877* (Tallahassee, Fla., 1965); Vernon Wharton, *The Negro in Mississippi, 1865-1890* (Chapel Hill, N.C., 1947). See also Martin Abbott, *The Freedmen's Bureau in South Carolina, 1865-1872* (Chapel Hill, N.C., 1967) and Howard A. White, *The Freedmen's Bureau in Louisiana* (Baton Rouge, 1970). Robert Cruden, *The Negro in Reconstruction* (New York, 1969) is a sound general account, and the earlier works of W.E. Burghardt DuBois, James S. Allen, and Alrutheus A. Taylor remain invaluable.

sophisticated, but it was nonetheless real. Freed people wandered in search of independence, families, and jobs; they selected names for themselves; they settled down to toil; they paid taxes for the first time; and they paid to legalize marriages and families that sometimes spanned generations. Not only did they meet needs and obligations with undeniable success, they began to recognize and demand their rights. Encouraged by the Freedmen's Bureau, they fought employers in thousands of instances for better contracts and fair treatment, and they carried whites before the courts for violating labor agreements and even for refusing to support children they had fathered. More able or fortunate freedmen staked homesteads or saved enough to purchase land. A few served as plantation managers or in other honored posts, and some of the skilled or clever launched professional or business careers of their own. But while individuals benefited and a talented and propertied class grew, the vast bulk of the freed population found little if any immediate economic advantage in freedom. Prejudice and persisting disadvantages, including the lasting poverty of a disrupted and underdeveloped region, kept the black population an impoverished and mistreated laboring group. It remains unclear to what extent radical Reconstruction may have made that socioeconomic status a bit more favorable than it might otherwise have been.[10]

There were other areas of black progress too. The federal government, idealistic Yankee emissaries, and sympathetic southerners expended much time and energy in promoting education, while blacks responded eagerly with students, schools, money, and teachers of their own. To escape discrimination, blacks also often broke away from whites to establish churches, celebrations, and social organizations of their own, thus contributing to a growing pattern of racial separation that was being demanded for other reasons by their foes. Black aspirations also reached beyond emancipation in an open struggle against racial inequalities and prejudice. Prominent in that struggle was an emerging black upper class of teachers, preachers, former soldiers, and successful farmers, artisans, and small business men.

Reflecting their own success and the phenomenal accomplishments of the Civil War, black leaders displayed a great faith in the American system. They appeared radical only on the question of race, and their ideology was characterized by a pragmatic modera-

[10] Joel Williamson challenges the traditional assumption in concluding that radical Reconstruction made the situation of southern blacks more favorable than it would otherwise have been. *After Slavery*, p. 179.

tion that fully endorsed the values of free enterprise and the political party system. While more radical desires, particularly for the confiscation and distribution of land, existed among the mass of freed people and received some expression, the most familiar and persuasive demand presented by black spokesmen was one for the same political and legal rights, the same opportunities, and the same advantages and disadvantages that prevailed among whites. [11] This demand, which was also being voiced by radical Republicans in the North, furnished much of the rationale for the Reconstruction settlement of 1867.

As indicated earlier, northern Republicans remained dissatisfied with developments in the South during 1865 and 1866. Also fearful that a new national political alliance might displace them from control of the federal government, they blocked reunion until an acceptable postwar settlement could be achieved. Late in 1866, Congress offered some promise of such a settlement in the proposed Fourteenth Amendment, the crucial sections of which promised federal protection of southern blacks and Unionists, barred certain Confederates from office, and reduced southern representation in the national government until the freedmen were enfranchised by the states. This moderate offer was overwhelmingly rejected by all of the Confederate states except Tennessee, which was shortly readmitted to the Union. Convinced that the remainder of the former Confederacy remained dangerously defiant and that more severe steps were in order, Congress now attempted to guarantee the victory and aims of the Republican party by enfranchising the freedmen of those states. In addition, certain distrusted whites were momentarily disfranchised and military supremacy was restored until the new program had been satisfactorily carried out. In the evolution of this policy, more radical proposals for the confiscation and distribution of land to provide freedmen with the wherewithal to succeed were defeated, as were proposals for a more extended period of federal tutelage and protection.

Despite its imposition of black suffrage and a temporary military supremacy, this radical Reconstruction program of 1867 constituted a poorly conceived effort to end rather than perpetuate northern interference in the South, an effort that served the

---

[11] Various Negro conventions in both North and South make this clear, the North Carolina convention of 1865 being so cautious as not to request the vote. Herbert Aptheker (ed.), *A Documentary History of the Negro People in the United States* (New York, 1951), pp. 507-547.

immediate needs of the North while forcing a new tragedy upon the suffering South. In essence, Republicans sought to wash their hands of an embarrassing southern problem by extending the vote to blacks and then leaving blacks and their allies pretty much to fend for themselves. While such an approach accorded well with the demands of federalism and the highly touted spread of manhood suffrage during the earlier Jacksonian age, it did not accord well with the realities of American racism or the total situation in the South. A highly volatile race issue had been introduced into politics, and southern blacks and their allies were ill prepared for the tasks they faced. The new voters were deplorably poor, illiterate, and inexperienced; reliable allies of the appropriate commitment and ability were rare; and practically all levels of economic and social power were dominated by the opposition. Northern Republicans had been deluded by their faith in the power of the vote and the workings of the electoral system, and, when southern politics did not proceed as was expected, the nation's commitment to federalism would preclude the vigorous national role required.

Nevertheless, in response to the Reconstruction program, Republican parties were established throughout the former Confederacy. In a marked transformation of political power, they captured control first of the Reconstruction process and then of the state governments for varying lengths of time everywhere except in Virginia. Dependent primarily upon the Negro vote, these Republican parties were also significantly supported and, in the main, led by southern whites and recent immigrants from the North. Apparently, most native white Republicans were poorer workers and farmers who possessed a long record of opposition to the former Confederate and slaveholding gentry which had continued to dominate the postwar South.[12] This record included bitter opposition to the war and an older hankering for democratic reform in a South where such reform had often lagged. Also inclined toward Republicanism were cultivated southerners of nationalist, liberal, or moderate views, many of whom had been Unionists or Whigs sympathetic to the economic nationalism of the Republican party. Some native Republicans attributed the

[12] For the still disputed question of scalawags see David Donald, "The Scalawag in Mississippi Reconstruction," *Journal of Southern History* X (1944), pp. 447-60; Allen W. Trelease, "Who Were the Scalawags?" *ibid.*, XXIX (1963), pp. 445-68; David Donald's reply to Trelease, *ibid.*, XXX (1964), pp. 253-57; Warren A. Ellem, "Who Were the Mississippi Scalawags?" *ibid.*, XXXVIII (1972), pp. 217-40.

forlorn condition of the South to rulers who deserved repudiation; some were tolerant of racial and political reform; and some were anxious to guide this powerful new force into moderate channels. There were also many supporters who hoped to effect little more than restoration as a necessary prelude to ending federal intervention and reestablishing former rule.[13] As for recent Yankee immigrants, men following one of the most familiar paths of the American experience—migration—they usually brought their Republicanism from home and varied greatly in their definition of that term.

It was, however, the freedman voter who constituted the real substance of Republican strength in the South, and there was something astonishing in the effectiveness with which the former slave population was organized to take advantage of its newfound power. Illiteracy and ignorance were prevalent among these new voters, although these faults were also common among southern whites; and there was an element of regimentation in their political methods which reflected not only their limitations but their conscious desires and needs as well. Many of the issues were all too clear, and to a large extent freedmen entered upon their political duties with an enthusiastic awareness of what they were about.

Insofar as it was primarily dependent upon Negro voters, this truly was a Black Reconstruction, although in the long run the voting support of a white minority was imperative in all but the two states where blacks constituted a majority of the population. Furthermore, the leadership of southern Republican governments remained overwhelmingly white. Blacks held no governorship, only one state supreme court post, and few cabinet and congressional posts; only South Carolina ever had a black majority in a branch of the legislature, the lower house. Nevertheless, there was a sudden and surprising emergence of black political leaders on the local, state, and national level, from local Union League and party leaders to policemen and justices of the peace, from state legislators to lieutenant governors and two Senators of the United States. The more impressive black leaders usually boasted prewar accomplishments or education, but many others had just emerged from slavery or an obscure antebellum freedom. On the whole, black

[13] Richmond M. Pearson, Republican Chief Supreme Court Justice of North Carolina, publicly wrote: "When the storm is over, the Conservative party, representing as it does, the property and intelligence of the State, will take the guidance of affairs, and all will be well." Raleigh *Standard*, August 11, 1868.

leaders appeared characterized by moderation, perhaps excessively so; they also stumbled and fell and could hardly be expected to stand equally in knowledge or skill with more informed and experienced whites. But they did know something of the needs of their people; they suffered primarily from limitations not of their own making; and their performance often compared remarkably well with that of their white allies and foes.[14]

The high point of southern Republican accomplishment and success occurred in the first years of Reconstruction, when the party captured control of the required constitutional conventions and rewrote the fundamental law of every reconstructed state. This first test of the wisdom of black suffrage and Republicanism resulted in constitutions that were a decisive improvement over those of the past and which were characterized by such significant reforms as the establishment of a state system of public schools, legal and penal reform, the abolition of imprisonment for debt, labor liens and homesteads, increased public care for the indigent and handicapped, an increased separation of powers, more local self-government, and a more equitable shifting of the tax burden onto the wealthy.

To a conservative opposition, too impoverished and embittered to bear well the mental and economic costs involved, these constitutional changes appeared dangerously extreme, although they amounted to little more than a modernization already common to most of the United States. The rationale and accomplishment of Republicanism clearly reflected a familiar American economic and political view and was hardly revolutionary or peculiarly black in orientation. Furthermore, Republicans had proven extremely considerate of the privileges of property owners, had in almost every instance backed down on the explosive issue of integration, and, despite efforts in some states to do so, had not seriously restricted the equal rights of the opposition. Most of the constitutional changes accomplished proved so popular that they were eventually endorsed by the opposition and retained long beyond the collapse of Reconstruction.

The subsequent Republican governments in the South were less successful and enduring than the party's initial constitutional reforms. By 1870, all the former Confederate states had been

---

[14] For black political activity see especially Williamson, *After Slavery*; Richardson, *The Negro in the Reconstruction of Florida*; Peggy Lamson, *The Glorious Failure: Black Congressman Robert Brown Elliott and the Reconstruction in South Carolina* (New York, 1973).

restored to the Union, Virginia escaping a Republican regime altogether, while Republican control in varying degree lasted elsewhere for from one to nine years. The last states to be "redeemed" were Mississippi in 1875 and Louisiana, Florida, and South Carolina in 1877. One great difficulty in relating the political history of this entire experience is that it consists of the separate and varying tale of ten states, with those variations proceeding largely from differences in racial composition, existing economic and political conditions, state leadership, and fortuitous events. The element most obviously common to all of the states involved was the enduring unacceptability of Republican rule and Republican principles to an adamant, white supremacist opposition that dominated the power of the South and that was remarkably unrestrained in the nature of its resistance.

Those southern whites who were unwilling to endorse Republicanism or the principles of radical Reconstruction were befuddled and split in their initial response. Most remained identified with a Conservative or a Democratic party, with many temporarily sulking and avoiding political activity altogether and others half-heartedly wooing the new black voter. The entire proslavery past militated against this courtship as did its limited, paternalistic, and ultimately threatening nature. The South's former rulers soon discovered that the difficulty with poor and illiterate black voters was not that their vote could be controlled but that it could not be. Conservative-Democrats either would not or could not compete with Republican parties that not only boasted momentous accomplishments in the past but that also accorded a high degree of equal participation to blacks and advocated social and political reforms of significant benefit to the poor. As it became clear during 1867 that the freedmen overwhelmingly supported the only party offering them meaningful equality and gain and consequently that Republicans commanded a majority of the southern electorate, there occurred a fusion of wartime hatreds and political frustrations with class and racial fears that turned the bulk of the white leadership of the South adamantly against black voters and the southern Republican parties.

Because black suffrage did indeed bring about the intended defeat of the indigenous rulers of the South, the issue of self-determination was intensified. Not only was the black vote lost, but it was responsible for the success of a movement equated with racial insult, sectional humiliation, dangerous and costly innovation in state government, and the displacement of legitimate rulers by Yankees, inferiors, and traitors. The white leadership of the South responded by achieving a pervasive new political unity to fight against this purportedly illegal and immoral attempt to impose an alien regime upon the South.[15] Most of this leadership obviously consisted of former slaveholders, a large group constituting the most influential and wealthy one-third of the white population of the former Confederacy and which had a strong material and ideological commitment to the continued suppression of blacks.

Confirmed in their racism and their distrust of political democracy by the voting behavior of blacks, the opponents of Republicanism also found it politically expedient to direct their vengeance primarily against the troublesome Negro. Of course, the black vote already was almost solidly Republican, but Republicans needed and welcomed white support and leadership, and it was the opposition that chose to make the color line itself a political issue. The North Carolina Conservative party declaration of February 1868 typified the demand for white supremacy and the endless racist demagoguery that thereafter characterized Reconstruction political rivalry: "The great and all-absorbing issue, now soon to be presented to the people of the States, is negro suffrage and negro equality, if not supremacy, and whether hereafter in North Carolina and the South, the white man is to be placed politically, and as a consequence socially, upon a footing of equality with the negro."[16]

This racist appeal, designed to unify southern whites against Republicanism, was most useful and first successfully utilized in those states where blacks constituted a minority of the voting population. Eventually, other considerations were overshadowed elsewhere as well, and white supremacy became central to the redemption movement in all the reconstructed states.[17] The same leaders who had united southern whites successfully in support of

[15] Reflective of differences in principle and strategy the date and persistence of formal political unity varied. Because of a black voting majority, formal unity was not achieved in Mississippi until 1875, and, while achieved earlier in states such as North Carolina and Georgia, unity weakened in 1872.

[16] Raleigh *Sentinel*, February 7, 1868. The same stance was taken earlier in Georgia. See Conway, *Reconstruction of Georgia*, p. 152.

[17] The size and strength of the black population in South Carolina, Florida, Mississippi, and Louisiana occasioned unusual fluctuations in Conservative tactics. For the Mississippi case see Garner, *Reconstruction in Mississippi*, and William C. Harris, "The Collapse of the Reconstruction Order in Mississippi" (to be published).

slavery and the Confederacy now united them more successfully in support of white supremacy as the essence of home rule. It is true that racism was already deeply ingrained in southern, as well as national, life and that race consciousness was intensified in the South by the unusual presence of millions of degraded blacks and the variety of competitive threats they offered. Nevertheless, southern white Republicans suggested a racial adjustment to those conditions that does not appear to have been culturally unrealistic in its demands. What made it unrealistic in the last analysis was the total context in which those demands occurred. That context involved other issues as well as that of race but stimulated a political agitation that hardened and intensified the racist commitment of the white South.

During the first two years of radical Reconstruction, Conservative Democrats were severly handicapped by disunity, demoralization, and continuing federal intervention. In several states, however, they delayed the reconstruction process and defeated the attempted political proscription of former Confederates. Their stand was unusually extreme during 1868 when they condemned Negro suffrage and the Reconstruction acts as unconstitutional and called for their repeal through the election of a Democratic President. The election of Ulysses S. Grant dashed those hopes. Meanwhile, the more moderate opponents of Republicanism had urged an acceptance of the Reconstruction acts, anticipating a final settlement of internal politics only after restoration had been achieved. In accordance with that advice, the opponents of Republicanism united upon a milder position after Grant's election which was designed to discourage further federal intervention and achieve a broader anti-Republican unity within the South.

A clear distinction was now drawn between black rights and black power as Conservative-Democrats pledged their acceptance of equal rights together with their continuing determination to defeat black Republicanism and restore white rule. Throughout the remainder of Reconstruction, they labored to convince both southern whites and the North that Republican rule was opposed and deserved defeat primarily because it was notoriously inefficient and corrupt. Simultaneously, they promised that white supremacist parties and governments would fully honor the rights of blacks and all federal Reconstruction legislation. Unfortunately, such assurances were but one side of an amazingly effective political strategy that had another vicious side. Too often, Conservative-Democrats had little real respect for blacks or their rights, and racist demagoguery and various forms of extremism typified their operations.

The almost total domination of southern power by the opponents of Republicanism enabled them to proceed with great effectiveness. They controlled the overwhelming proportion of the wealth, land, experience, talent, and press facilities. They dominated the legal, business, and professional classes, as well as the churches, the college-educated population, the social organizations, and the socioeconomic power structure at community, county, and state levels. In counties with substantial black populations, they included almost the entire white population, and they represented an ideological heritage, including more than white supremacy, that had never been effectively challenged. White Republicans, on the other hand, were predominantly identified as mavericks or with the poorer classes and regions of the South, although they were often individually prosperous and unusually strong among urban business groups.[18]

Reflective of their strength and anger, Conservative-Democrats opposed southern Republicans in a manner that made it impossible for either party politics or state governments to function in a reasonable manner. It was soon apparent that they sought to destroy rather than compete with Republicanism and that they were capable of utilizing any means considered necessary to do so. Irresponsible race demagoguery was constant and intense. Intimidation and violence, including murder, were common from the early appearance of the Ku Klux Klan to the rifle clubs and red shirts of 1876. Campaign tools included legal harassment, economic discrimination and reprisal, social ostracism, and even exclusion from church and communion. Stuffed ballot boxes, fraudulent counts, and other forms of trickery characterized elections, and Conservative-Democratic victories were followed by flagrant gerrymandering, partisan trials and impeachment proceedings, and election laws discriminating against the poor. The entire process established habits of gross political immorality that would plague the South for decades.[19]

[18] They by no means dominated the business element. William McKee Evans, *Ballots and Fence Rails: Reconstruction on the Lower Cape Fear,* pp. 124-25, 163. The impressive wealth and intellect of Republican leaders does not negate the basic poverty of the party and its supporters.

[19] Traditionalists admitted as much, e.g.: "The practical necessities of the case overcame scrupulous nations of political morality, and a determination to rule by any means possible possessed the mass of the white people and held them during the

In practically every political realm, Conservative-Democrats proved far more imaginative, daring, and astute than their opponents. While encouraging and reaping the rewards of extremism and violence, they were masters at periodically presenting a moderate image either for northern consumption or the encouragement of Republican factionalism at home. Even when such variations were sincerely based, the diverse opponents of Republicanism displayed a remarkable ability to unite on election day because they were united in a basic opposition to the legitimacy of southern Republicanism.

Redemption propaganda was irresponsible and overwhelming. Hardly a mistake was made by Republicans that the redeemers would not, could not, and did not capitalize upon. When mistakes were not forthcoming, rumors, half-truths, and lies were assiduously circulated to build a lasting web of slander and distortion. In this fashion, Republicans were abused and confounded and ultimately made scapegoats for almost all of the ills of the South, including those left by the war, and a myth was created which unified the whites and became the substance of a false but lasting Reconstruction legend.[20]

The lasting stereotypes of scalawag, carpetbagger, and vicious black and the terrible nature of Republicanism were false. In general, Republican leaders were neither racial, political, nor economic extremists, nor were they blatantly evil or corrupt. They were usually reasonable and enlightened men who endorsed a free-enterprise system that accorded ordinary civil and political equality to blacks and who supported moderate reforms that had already been accepted in most of the United States. In some obvious respects, Republicans were more conservative than their opponents; and no matter how illiterate and inexperienced black voters were, the officials they helped elect were on the whole neither vicious nor totally incompetent. Conservatives were unable or unwilling to make that admission or to allow a continuing fair test.

Of course, the opponents of Republicanism were convinced of the substance of their discontent. Emancipation, black suffrage, federal intervention, political upheaval, and the assertiveness of

---

following three decades. That they were right is not to be doubted in the face of the facts, but it must nevertheless continue to be a cause of regret that such a thing was necessary to secure good government." J. G. deRoulhac Hamilton, *Reconstruction in North Carolina* (New York, 1914), p. 422.

[20] Olsen, *Carpetbagger's Crusade*, pp. 148-52; Albert T. Morgan, *Yazoo: Or, on the Picket Line of Freedom in the South* (Washington, D.C., 1884), ch. 68-72

poor whites and "uppity" blacks did rankle, and, in many counties, racially sensitive whites were deeply offended by black majority control. The establishment of public schools and new social services together with lavish grants to railroads did increase taxes, and those taxes were levied more heavily than before upon land. Increased government services were justifiable, however, and the much condemned railroad projects, which were considered necessary to the economic development of the South, were undertaken with extensive Conservative-Democratic support. As for the grossly exaggerated Reconstruction state debts, they did not prove much of a burden to the South because they were repudiated by the redeemers and in a fashion that probably did more harm to southern credit than the initial debt itself.

There was, it is true, Republican incompetence, waste, and fraud that merited condemnation. But these were not sins peculiar to Reconstruction Republicanism. They were and have remained common faults of state governments throughout the history of the United States. For example, the stealing by the Tweed ring in New York alone during this period apparently exceeded that by all of the southern Republican governments combined, but only in the South were such occurrences utilized as an excuse for totally discrediting manhood suffrage and undermining the democratic political process. Furthermore, while some Reconstruction state governments (those in South Carolina and Louisiana) have retained the reputation of being unusually corrupt, others (those in Florida, North Carolina, and Mississippi) have been judged more constructive or honest than the white supremacist governments that preceded or followed Republican rule.[21] One should also note that southern Republicanism imposed no burden on the South, financial or otherwise, comparable to that imposed by those who brought on the Civil War.

It was, in fact, the impact of the Civil War that created a number of crucial Republican problems. For example, Republicans were challenging a tradition of minimal state government at a time when the burden of doing so had become unusually great. Emancipation had increased the free citizenry of the former Confederacy by over a third, thus necessitating a corresponding increase in many government services and costs which were further enlarged by Republican enthusiasm for reform and internal im-

[21] Richardson, *The Negro in the Reconstruction of Florida*, pp. 204-6, 223-24; Wharton, *The Negro in Mississippi*, pp. 170-72, 179; Olsen, *Carpetbagger's Crusade*, pp. 127-129, 140-142.

provements. At the same time, the tremendous destruction and loss of southern wealth lessened the ability to meet such expenses and presented additional recovery costs. A drop in property values to a third or a half of prewar figures meant a doubling or tripling of taxes merely to hold to former revenue levels. It is true that Reconstruction taxes usually were not high compared to taxes in other states, but they were many times increased over the past and thus new to the South at a moment when they were particularly difficult to bear. An upturn in southern economic conditions at the time Republicans first assumed power proved temporary, and economic difficulties were increasingly intensified by the disadvantageous position of an agricultural South in an industrial age. National economic crises in 1869 and 1873 contributed to the disastrous collapse of Republican railroad projects, and there was little sympathy from a North still distrustful of the South and committed to the doctrines of laissez-faire.

The real heart of the Republican dilemma was, however, an intrinsic weakness that was the reverse side of the opposition's strength. The success of a political movement as radical as that represented by southern Republicanism required an indigenous development that simply had not occurred. Having been created and placed in power by the external force of the North, southern Republicanism commanded but a minute proportion of the South's ability and power, and it lacked the unity, strength, and tradition to maintain itself.

While it is true that there often was strong, even majority, voting support for the Republican party, the realities of politics demanded much more. There had been no natural development of party organization, leadership, or goals. Most southern Republican leaders stepped forward to control a situation they had played little part in creating and to urge the acceptance of principles they had never before endorsed. Almost no native white Republican previously had endorsed political equality for blacks, and the cultural and communication gap between black and white was immense. The top levels of white leadership consisted largely of naive idealists or unusually liberal southerners who were embarrassed and apologetic from the very first, while the party's sudden origins and need of leadership elevated more than the usual share of incompetents and opportunists. The organizational accomplishments of the Union Leagues during 1867 and 1868 could not remedy such weaknesses. In fact, this remarkable mobilization of voters, mostly black, generated mass aspirations and radical demands that soon clashed with the cautious political pragmatism of a liberal, upper-class leadership that was responsible for much of the early Republican success.

Frightened and embarrassed by their principles, their mistakes, and their weaknesses, Republican leaders were seldom very aggressive after 1868.[22] They were very much men of moderation and reasonable persuasion rather than of radicalism or power, something attributable both to the type of liberal attitude that had acquiesced to federal demands in the first place and the limited affinity between the leadership and the predominantly black voting base. Time and again Republicans appeared to be pleading for an acceptance of their principles and existence rather than imposing them through the kind of power struggle typical of radical historical change. To a surprising extent this supposedly radical movement was actually characterized by timidity and by racial, political, and economic orthodoxy. It has even been suggested that the key weaknesses of southern Republicanism were not that it was so corrupt but that it was so honest, not that it was evil but that it was idealistic and naive, not that it was extreme but that it was conciliatory and proper, and not that it was committed to racial equality but that it was not.[23]

Once beyond their initial successes, Republicans were ineffective in developing a program to inspire continuing mass support. Having expected a restoration of normal political rivalries under newly imposed conditions, they were bewildered by the intransigent determination of their opponents to destroy them. In their frustration, they were beset by divisions catering to their foes, as native fought with carpetbagger, moderate with radical, and white with black. Some whites were obviously deserting the party because of the effectiveness of racist propaganda or the increasing aspirations among blacks for a more equitable share of Republican offices, while there were also blacks who concluded that the realities of the situation justified an alignment with the redeemers.

Admitting these Republican weaknesses, it is not clear that

[22] Conway, *Reconstruction in Georgia*, p. 223; Richardson, *The Negro in the Reconstruction of Florida*, pp. 225-26.

[23] Otto H. Olsen, "Reconsidering the Scalawags," *Civil War History* XII (1966), pp. 316-20. For example, Republican Governors William W. Holden of North Carolina and Daniel H. Chamberlain of South Carolina were hostile to black equality. W. W. Holden to Raleigh *News and Observer*, August 31, 1883; William W. Holden Papers, Duke University Library; Hampton M. Jarrell, *Wade Hampton and the Negro: The Road Not Taken* (Columbia, S. C., 1950), p. 44.

there then was any feasible alternative. Southern society was not prepared to submit to Republicanism or equal rights, and blacks and their allies were not equipped to win. Perhaps on the whole, Republicans did as well as could be expected. They came remarkably close to enduring success in a number of states, and they certainly made positive and lasting contributions to the South. The odds against them were simply too great.

The persistent problem of Reconstruction violence well illustrates Republican ineffectiveness at the state and national levels in coping with those odds. Between 1868 and 1871, thousands of beatings and other atrocities and hundreds of murders were attributable to a variety of secret organizations generally designated as the Ku Klux Klan.[24] These outrages were almost entirely directed against politically active blacks and their closest allies or other challengers to white supremacy. While motivated by a wide range of racial, economic, political, and even personal considerations, there can be no doubt that this terrorism was a central part of the total struggle against Republicanism in the South.

Perhaps the Klan can best be described as a clandestine guerrilla movement dedicated to the destruction of an alien regime and the restoration of white supremacy and home rule. Cowardly, racist, and cruel in its operations, the Klan showed twisted idealism in its defiance of the law and the North. Klansmen were convinced of the sanctity of white supremacy and home rule, and their leaders were prominent and respected men. Typical of members of guerrilla movements, Klansmen were locally autonomous and found needed support among the white population in those areas where they were most active. There was an obvious connection in membership and leadership between the Klan and the Conservative-Democratic parties, but, because of the criminal nature of the Klan and the opposition of moderates, that connection was neither formal nor admitted.

Retaliation discouraged Klan activity in areas of large black population, and there was successful resistance elsewhere; but too often Republicans were unable to protect themselves, and legal authorities were constantly baffled. The atrocities were committed by large bodies of fully disguised men, often from a distant locality, at night, and against one or few individuals, thus minimizing the chances of identification or resistance. Witnesses were intimidated or killed. Police and other local authorities were

[24] A good scholarly account of the Klan has finally been provided by Allen W. Trelease, *White Terror: The Ku Klux Klan Conspiracy and Southern Reconstruction* (New York, 1971).

sometimes Klan members. When identifications were ventured, Klansmen and their sympathizers appeared as attorneys, jurors, and false witnesses to thwart attempted prosecutions. Not only was the Klan destroying Republican leadership, principally at the local level, but, by exposing the inability of Republican governments to protect person and property, it contributed to the declining appeal of Reconstruction in the South and its ultimate abandonment by the North.

Failing in their efforts to prevent or prosecute Klan crime, Republican leaders continued to proclaim their full faith in the forces of law and to counsel their own suffering followers against private retaliation. Republican legislation and law enforcement lacked vigor, and Republican state officials were unwilling to utilize black troops, often the only available force, against suspected white Klansmen. Ostensibly, Republican leaders feared both failure and a further incitement of emotional racism, but victory in the Civil War itself had required a willingness to fight arm-in-arm with blacks, and southern Republican failure may have turned upon an unwillingness to do the same. At times, overly cautious Republican authorities even disbanded local black militia forces, only to pave the way for additional assassination.

Republicans relied primarily upon appeasement and conciliatory pleas to combat the Klan. They begged for aid in bringing an end to such violence, offered pardons for past crimes as an inducement for cooperation, and even disbanded the perfectly legitimate Union Leagues to placate their foes. Clearly, such timidity was incommensurate with governmental authority and the proper enforcement of the law, and as might have been anticipated Republican concessions were exploited without any significant returns. The entire situation testified to the fundamentally inadequate social base of the southern Republican party and left Republicans pleading in desperation for federal military aid.

The North was appalled at Klan violence but also exasperated at the inability of southern Republican governments to maintain order themselves. A renewal of federal military interference in the South would conflict with honored principles of civil supremacy and states' rights, and, while the military was prepared to deal with open rebellion, it was confused by the guerrilla tactics of the Klan. When federal troops were dispatched into an area of Klan activity, the organization simply curtailed its operations. Law and order thus appeared restored; the troops were withdrawn; and the

Klan remained free to reappear as the occasion arose. Since the authority of the federal government to intervene in criminal matters of this nature was unclear, the Grant administration urged a vigorous state militia response while promising to support state authorities if they were met by open resistance. When Republican states reluctantly did attempt such action, however, as in North Carolina during 1870, it proved ineffective and politically harmful.

The North finally was prompted to stringent measures. Congress conducted revealing investigations and passed new laws, and, during 1871 and 1872, federal arrests and prosecutions culminated in some convictions and the disappearance of the Ku Klux Klan. This severity was then replaced by a conciliatory program of pardon and amnesty, which in itself was an admission that the problems of neither southern Republicanism nor Reconstruction violence had truly been solved. In many states, the Klan simply was no longer needed. Republican power already had been eroded, and less drastic tactics were usually sufficient. Coercion and violence periodically did reappear, however, and were very evident in 1875 and 1876 in those states with the largest black populations and strongest Republican parties—Mississippi, Louisiana, Florida, and South Carolina. Once again, white Republican governors proved reluctant to utilize black troops or were finagled out of doing so by empty opposition promises, while the federal government avoided direct intervention, complained of repeated southern disorder, and vacillated in its advice. Accordingly, the final overthrow of southern Republicanism during these years was accompanied by extensive intimidation and violence, although no longer in the garb of the Ku Klux Klan.[25]

From 1868 to 1876, southern Republican strength had steadily waned despite the fact that Republican parties sometimes did function with substantial effectiveness beyond their initial electoral defeat. Following the crushing of the Klan and the moderating impact of the liberal Republican movement upon Conservative-Democratic tactics, new Republican victories were achieved in Alabama and North Carolina in 1872. Nevertheless, at the end of 1876, the white supremacist redeemers claimed political control in every one of the former Confederate states. The affirmation of that control in three states and the freedom with which it would

[25] Wharton, *The Negro in Mississippi*, ch. 13; Richardson, *The Negro in the Reconstruction of Florida*, pp. 236-37; Francis B. Simkins and Robert H. Woody, *South Carolina During Reconstruction* (Chapel Hill, N.C., 1932), ch. 18; Ella Lonn, *Reconstruction in Louisiana after 1868* (New York, 1918), pp. 412-19.

be consolidated throughout the South were entwined with efforts at the national level to resolve the disputed presidential election of 1876. The resolution of that dispute culminated in the North's abandonment of radical Reconstruction.

By 1877, the postwar fear and idealism of the North had dwindled away, and that section had become increasingly weary of the southern problem and preoccupied with the promise and problems of the industrial age. The northern Republican party had fallen into the hands of business-oriented leaders who, like southern redeemers, believed in the power and privileges of wealth, were unsympathetic to radicalism of any sort, and thought that economic development was being discouraged by continuing disorder in the South. It was now clear that the more obvious desires of the North were safely secured, that southern Republicanism was a constantly disrupting force, and that national harmony might be more thoroughly achieved by catering to the white supremacist South. Southern redeemers catered to this opportunity with professions of proper loyalty and economic principles as well as with promises to protect the constitutional rights of socially inferior and thoroughly dominated blacks.

The stage was thus set for the new expedient consensus achieved by the "reunion and reaction" of 1877. The North obtained the Presidency and the promise of stability and a more acceptable southern attitude. The South was granted home rule at the somewhat obscured expense of scalawags, carpetbaggers, and blacks. Confirmed in their control of the South and in an end to federal interference, the redeemers then proceeded to ensure the permanence of white supremacy and Democratic rule and to perpetuate a view of Reconstruction justifying that triumph. Although Republican strength in the South still offered the promise of meaningful two-party politics, that promise was rapidly undermined by the determination to travel the road of white supremacy and one-party rule.

The sources of the ultimate collapse of radical Reconstruction did not rest in either the supposed incapacity of black voters or in Republican corruption and misrule. They rested rather in a conflict between the cultural conditions and postwar expectations of the North and the South. The North had been remarkably incoherent in its demands, and the indigenous leadership of the South had remained so wedded to former interests and beliefs as to prevent a reasonable accommodation to the postwar situation that might have minimized the difficulties and maximized the benefits of either emancipation or equal rights. Southern leaders helped provoke a Reconstruction settlement that proved unwise, and they then tied the South to racism, reaction, and political immorality in an ironic triumph for home rule that deserved little of its traditional identification with purity and light.

It would appear in retrospect that, if the victorious North could use the war together with persuasions of justice and national loyalty as an excuse for so thoroughly disrupting the cultural situation within the South, these same arguments should also have been used to justify procedures guaranteeing success. But this did not happen. Instead, black suffrage and southern Republicanism were expected to succeed on their own, although in origin and essence they were far too extraneous to the cultural condition of the South to do so. The drama that unfolded had all the dimensions of classic tragedy. There were black and white heroes aplenty, a courageous battle against great wrong, and predestined, disastrous failure. The personal and impersonal sources of that failure were many, but they all flowed from the artificial essence of the entire effort.

The radical Reconstruction program was in basic conflict with the social reality of the South. It was not one of the recognized fruits of northern military victory, and it had all the appearances of an attempt at colonial domination. Southern Republicans could not overcome the cultural conditions they faced, and continuing federal attempts to keep them in power were inconsistent with the federal structure of a nation in which the South was supposed to be an equal. When the lapse of time revealed that the Reconstruction program was not necessary to the security of the United States, it was inconsistent with that security for the federal government to continue in a different relationship to the southern states than to other states of the Union. The maintenance of the Reconstruction program demanded a continuing federal role that conflicted not only with the accepted rights of states but also with the prevalent social philosophy of the day and the very idea of a truly successful reunion.

As for the overwhelming majority of the indigenous white leadership of the South, it was so intensely convinced of the alien essence of Republicanism, in both racial and political terms, that it submerged existing antagonisms in a new unity designed to eliminate this alien force as a meaningful element in the history of the South. Foreign intervention and outside agitators were infuriating realities to the white South, and the success of the redeemers was phenomenal. They not only achieved their political ends, they established a lasting new conformity in the white mind of the South and fashioned a rationale for their success that became one of the most enduring myths in national history. Perhaps the crowning irony was that in a very real sense Republicanism was not as alien as the redeemers insisted. After all, Republicans often did command majority support in the South; but the claim of that black and white majority to southern citizenship really was never conceded; a fact which in itself was another reflection of the extent to which Reconstruction was in fact foreign to the southern scene.

Traditional condemnations of radical Reconstruction invariably have touched upon its alien nature, but they have obscured that issue by focusing primarily upon such now discredited accusations as corruption and incompetence, disreputable carpetbaggers and scalawags, and the barbarism of black rule. In response, the defenders of Reconstruction have been so satisfied with their exposure of the racist and reactionary principles of the redeemers and the accomplishments of the Republicans that they have seldom considered the propriety or wisdom of this degree of northern interference in the internal affairs of the South. This latter issue most obviously involves the question of states' rights, but the southern conception of home rule encompassed more than this. It encompassed a general principle of self-determination that had a very deep meaning to the defeated South. The crucial question about all of this may be not how good or bad the Reconstruction governments were, nor even how much popular support they had, but whether or not they adequately corresponded to the indigenous condition of the post-Civil War South.

It cannot be denied that there has been something unusually distinctive about the South, although the precise meaning of that distinctiveness remains disputed. Scholars have perceived the South as a unique section, region, colony, and conglomeration of people or states, and they have identified it with a distinct mind, myth, mystique, hegemony, and historical experience. They have also devoted extensive attention to the development of a separate southern identity both before and since the Civil War, and sometimes they have even referred to that identity as southern nationalism. But historians have paid little attention to the relationship of this remarkable cultural independence to Reconstruction history, except insofar as they have pointed to racial peculiarities or to the manner in which Reconstruction itself created the solid South.[26] But the reality of a distinct South preceded and provoked and then defeated the Reconstruction plans of the North. Racial composition and attitudes formed a major part but not the whole of that distinct South.

That the United States has hesitated to recognize, let alone honor, the concept of southern sovereignty, even when it fell within the generally accepted realm of states' rights, is not surprising. The Civil War had been fought over too closely related a claim. The victors were unwilling to extend recognition to either the principle or the fact of what they had so narrowly defeated at such enormous cost, and that unwillingness has continued to protect the hallowedness of the Union cause. Recent revisionists have had even less regard for a concept of southern sovereignty that was also identified with white racism and the defeat of an equalitarian Reconstruction. As for the vanquished white southerners, they soon appreciated the disadvantages of presenting their claims in such a form, although their sentiments were quietly expressed by the ever-mounting numbers of Confederate monuments that graced cemeteries and city squares throughout the South. When other grounds of accommodation were found, both the Union and the requisite sovereignty of the southern states were preserved. The rights of blacks were easily ignored, and whatever claim they may have had to a doubly entrapped nationalism of their own was hardly even noted.

[26] Southern nationalism is well analyzed in Hans Kohn, *American Nationalism: An Interpretive Essay* (New York, 1957), pp. 107-22; and a shrewd originality was brought to that topic in David Potter, *The South and the Sectional Conflict* (Baton Rouge, 1968), ch. 3.

Selected Bibliography

The following short list of books is limited to studies that have special relevance to the essays in this volume. For an extensive bibliography covering all aspects of the Civil War and Reconstruction, see J. G. Randall and David Donald, *The Civil War and Reconstruction*, 2nd ed. rev. (Boston: D. C. Heath, 1969), pp. 703-834.

Berwanger, Eugene H., *The Frontier Against Slavery: Western Anti-Negro Prejudice and the Slavery Extension Controversy* (Urbana, Ill.: University of Illinois Press, 1967).

Brock, W. R., *An American Crisis: Congress and Reconstruction, 1865-1867* (New York: St. Martin's Press, 1963).

Cash, W. J., *The Mind of the South* (New York: Vintage Books, 1960).

Channing, Steven A., *Crisis of Fear: Secession in South Carolina* (New York: Simon and Schuster, 1970).

Craven, Avery, *The Coming of the Civil War*, 2nd ed. rev. (Chicago: University of Chicago Press, 1957).

——, *The Growth of Southern Nationalism, 1848-1861* (Baton Rouge: Louisiana State University Press, 1953).

Cruden, Robert, *The Negro in Reconstruction* (Englewood Cliffs, N.J.: Prentice-Hall, 1969).

Donald, David, *Lincoln Reconsidered*, 2nd ed. enlarged (New York: Vintage Books, 1956).

——, ed., *Why the North Won the Civil War* (New York: Collier Books, 1962).

Du Bois, W. E. B., *Black Reconstruction in America, 1860-1880* (New York: Atheneum, 1970).

Fehrenbacher, Don E., *Prelude to Greatness: Lincoln in the 1850's* (Stanford, Calif.: Stanford University Press. 1962).

Foner, Eric, *Free Soil, Free Labor, Free Men: The Ideology of the Republican Party before the Civil War* (New York: Oxford University Press, 1970).

Franklin, John Hope, *Reconstruction: After the Civil War* (Chicago: University of Chicago Press, 1961).

Fredrickson, George M., *The Inner Civil War: Northern Intellectuals and the Crisis of the Union* (New York: Harper and Row, 1965).

———. *The Black Image in the White Mind: The Debate on Afro-American Character and Destiny, 1817-1914* (New York: Harper and Row, 1971).

Freehling, William W., *Prelude to Civil War: The Nullification Controversy in South Carolina* (New York: Harper and Row, 1966.)

Gillette, William, *The Right to Vote: Politics and the Passage of the Fifteenth Amendment* (Baltimore: Johns Hopkins Press, 1965).

McKitrick, Eric L., *Andrew Johnson and Reconstruction* (Chicago: University of Chicago Press, 1960).

Nevins, Allan, *Ordeal of the Union,* 8 vols. (New York: Charles Scribner and Sons, 1947-1971).

Nichols, Roy Franklin, *The Disruption of American Democracy* (New York: Free Press Paperbacks, 1967).

Olsen, Otto H., *Carpetbagger's Crusade: The Life of Albion Winegar Tourgee* (Baltimore: Johns Hopkins Press, 1965).

Owsley, Frank Lawrence, *State Rights in the Confederacy* (Chicago: University of Chicago Press, 1925).

Perman, Michael, *Reunion Without Compromise: The South and Reconstruction, 1865-1868* (Cambridge: Cambridge University Press, 1973).

Potter, David M., *The South and the Sectional Conflict* (Baton Rouge: Louisiana State University Press, 1968).

Quarles, Benjamin, *Lincoln and the Negro* (New York: Oxford University Press, 1962).

Stampp, Kenneth M., *The Era of Reconstruction, 1865-1877* (New York: Knopf, 1965).

Sydnor, Charles, *The Development of Southern Sectionalism, 1819-1848* (Baton Rouge: Louisiana State University Press, 1948).

Thomas, Emory M., *The Confederacy as a Revolutionary Experience* (Englewood Cliffs, N. J.: Prentice-Hall, 1971).

Trefousse, Hans L., *The Radical Republicans: Lincoln's Vanguard for Racial Justice* (New York: Knopf, 1969).

Trelease, Allen W., *White Terror: The Ku Klux Klan Conspiracy and Reconstruction* (New York: Harper and Row, 1971).

Voegeli, V. Jacque, *Free but Not Equal: The Midwest and the Negro during the Civil War* (Chicago: University of Chicago Press, 1967).

Wharton, Vernon L., *The Negro in Mississippi, 1865-1890* (New York: Harper Torchbooks, 1965).

Wiley, Bell Irvin, *The Road to Appomattox* (New York: Atheneum, 1968).

Williamson, Joel, *After Slavery: The Negro in South Carolina During*

Reconstruction, 1861-1877 (Chapel Hill, N.C.: University of North Carolina Press, 1965).

Woodward, C. Vann, *American Counterpoint: Slavery and Racism in the North-South Dialogue* (Boston: Little, Brown, 1971).